Working with Reiki

Sarah Cooper

The author asserts the moral right under the Copyright, Designs and Patents Act 1988 to be identified as the author of this work.

All rights reserved. No part of this publication may be reproduced, stored in a retrieval system, or transmitted, in any form or means without the prior written consent of the publisher, nor be otherwise circulated in any form of binding or cover other than that in which it is published and without a similar condition being imposed on the subsequent purchaser.

Published in 2019 ☼

Copyright © Sarah Cooper

First Edition

ISBN-13: 978-1-0703-5772-0

Disclaimer

All of the information provided is being offered in good faith. However, neither the author nor publisher can accept any responsibility for the results of your actions in using any of the information contained in this book. Under no circumstances will any legal responsibility or blame be held against the author or publisher for any reparation, damages or monetary loss due to the information herein, either directly or indirectly.

Whilst the author has made every effort to provide you with the correct information, please note that it is your responsibility to ensure that you remain within the law in the areas in which you operate. Any advice or techniques suggested are given with the best intention, but it remains your responsibility to choose to accept them, or act upon them, and the author takes no responsibility in any way for the outcome of your doing so.

Reiki training and Reiki treatments should only ever be undertaken from those who can demonstrate the appropriate qualifications and adherence to legal requirements.

As with all complementary therapies, Reiki is not a substitute for proper medical diagnosis, or care from your GP. A Reiki treatment is not designed to diagnose a condition or prescribe medication. It is therefore recommended that you and your clients always consult a GP regarding an acute or infectious condition, and for any problems that in any way cause concern.

I dedicate this book to the love of my life,

Nic Cooper.

Thank you for accepting that your wife is

just a little on the weird side…

"I would rather have a mind opened by wonder than one closed by belief."

Gerry Spence

Acknowledgements

There are so many people whom I would wish to thank because in a way, if I have ever met you, you are someone who brought me to where I am now.

However, special mention must go to:

Caroline Tyler – you set me on my way with this and I can't thank you enough. The ability you have to shine in life has allowed me to find a way to shine myself.

Christina Cherry – you are amazing. Thank you so much for the time and effort you have put in on my behalf. A true friend.

Madeleine Foreman – I truly appreciate all of your help. Thank you.

Mark Wentworth – without your great wisdom and insight, my fingers would not have done this talking!

Steve Vince – for helping to bring this into reality.

And all those lovely people who have come to experience Reiki with me over the years. I value all that you have taught me, and hope that I have honoured our relationship by helping you in some small way too.

Contents

Reiki – A Personal View   1

In The Beginning

Starting Out   5
Your Equipment List   9
First Degree Reiki (Level One)   25
How Do You Do It?   37
Second Degree Reiki (Level Two)   47
Third Degree Reiki (Master Level)   51
Signs It's Working   59

Becoming Professional

Asking For Payment   71
Certification & Legislation   81
(Including Taxation, Lineage, & Music Licenses)
The Consultation   91
(Including Documentation & Data Protection)
Making An Appointment   113
Marketing   123

Challenges As You Progress

When Appointments Don't Go As Expected   135
(Small Things)
When Appointments Don't Go As Expected   151
(Some Bigger Things)
Reiki Is Change   177

Feeling Good Enough	187
The Importance Of Letting Go	209
What's There To Fear?	233
Client Feedback	247
Working With Young People	255

Some Final Thoughts

And Finally…	265

Reiki

Reiki is a very beautiful and special thing in my life. It is something that fills me with delight in its charmingly magical essence. It takes me to a place of wonder and yet a place of knowing. It feeds my very Soul. It is a reminder to me that despite our world being a place in which we see much to horrify and fill us with despair, the true foundation of life is pure love.

I cherish the fact that Reiki can be what you want and choose it to be, because Reiki only ever wants you to be who and what you are - your beautifully unique and individual self.

In one way it is simply a very practical tool for self-development and awareness, providing a framework in which to heal and bring life back into balance – whether the imbalance is for physical or emotional reasons, or (most usually) a combination of both. And yet in another, it can be an opening to your spiritual self, like a doorway to the part of you that somehow you feel but can't describe – that part which can feel tantalisingly close at certain times, and yet barely a distant memory at others.

Reiki is like a beacon of light in my life, strong, steady and constant. When the seas of life become turbulent and challenging, it is an ever-present force; bringing hope whilst guiding me out of the waves and back to calm waters. I love how it blends reconnection to our true spiritual nature with encouraging the emergence of our authentic personality, and in doing so brings more peace, love, joy and harmony whilst retaining a sense of humour along the way...

In The Beginning

Starting Out

Fabulous. If you're reading this then you are either connected with, or at the very least interested in, the wonderful world that is Reiki. And that gives me a beautifully warm feeling inside, because when you have a passion for something, there is a delight in sharing that passion with others.

Whether you are at the beginning of your Reiki journey and sensing the excitement of a new, and might I say rather magical, adventure, or whether you already have a degree of experience in the field, which is drawing you towards a deeper exploration, I hope this book will fulfil its intention. Its purpose being to provide you with friendly advice, support and inspiration.

Reiki courses usually consist of only a few days in the company of a teacher. Consequently many people are being given very little opportunity to work with the energy before they are faced with the client environment, even if those 'clients' are friends or members of your own family. With so little preparation, it is easy to see the value in supplementing your training by learning what it really means to be a Practitioner. After all, if you can avoid some pitfalls from the security of your reading chair, rather than in front of a client, that surely has to be a good thing hasn't it?

And to those of you who are already established Practitioners, I'm sure you'll agree that there is still much to be gained by learning from one another's experiences, leading us to greater understanding, and establishing improved ways in which to help the range of clients that walk through our door. Sharing our knowledge can be a very powerful thing.

So here's my aim: to help you to become the best Reiki Practitioner that you can be – because that's exactly what I wanted from the outset of my career, and still do to this day. And I would have loved the comfort of a book such as this to help me to get there.

However, you may be thinking there are many authors writing about Reiki (you'd be right), making you wonder why you should read this.

Well, the reason is, I felt compelled to write a book owing to what I saw was lacking in others. Because understanding someone's interpretation about what Reiki is and how it was founded, being taught which hand positions may benefit particular conditions, and establishing how chakras and meridians could become relevant, is really only part of the story. And I'm guessing these are the things you have already learnt, or will be learning, no matter how thorough your training. In my experience, these are also the topics covered in the majority of Reiki books, and are readily available online.

What I found was missing was the emotional perspective of being a Practitioner, and if you intend working for both your and your client's highest good, I would suggest that mastering your thoughts and emotions about yourself will prove to be key foundations in ensuring you attain the best results you can.

In this book, therefore, my objective is to help you overcome the doubts and fears that working in such an unfamiliar field often brings. It being a good bet that I've experienced enough of them to cover the majority of those that you'll come up against!

That's why as well as discussing the practical implications, such as data protection, music licenses and what to include in a well-structured treatment, we'll also consider things like how to improve your levels of trust in the energy; how to cope when appointments don't appear to be going as planned; how to value your time sufficiently to feel at ease in charging for your services; and how to develop the art of keeping strong, positive and focused, even when an individual's response to Reiki has been less than ideal.

Additionally, I want to give comfort, support and motivation to any of you who have walked away from your First Degree (level one) course, feeling as though you are unable to connect to this beautiful energy. I want to let you know how, for such a natural thing, it came anything but naturally to me. If you have been telling yourself that you can't do it, or that it won't work for you because whilst everyone around you seems to sense it, you…well…don't. Then I want to encourage you to persevere. Understand that this is purely the starting point of your Reiki journey. It has nothing at all to do with where you will end up.

I have included aspects of my personal training journey to inspire those of you who struggle initially. Please keep going – you are not alone.

Your Equipment List

The easiest way to remember how to pronounce Reiki is to think of 'Rei' as being like a 'ray' of light, which seems highly appropriate since many sense Reiki as beautiful light filling their body. 'Ki' like a 'key' that unlocks a door. Again very apt, since Reiki so often acts as a starting point to unlocking our self-awareness. In doing so it allows us to find more opportunities for inner peace, balance and well-being.

Reiki is mostly commonly translated from its original Japanese as 'universal, life-force energy'. It can be difficult to define, not least because generally it is something to be experienced and felt, (rather than read about and learnt). Sometimes it appears destined to remain beyond our total understanding – part of the mystery of life.

That's particularly hard when you begin, because there's just going to be you and an energy you can't fully describe, and certainly can't (and shouldn't) feel in control of. In most other professions, there is something else to support you, or to introduce to your clients either to spark their interest, or possibly even distract them; something that you can hide behind or outwardly promote. Most jobs at the very least will provide you with the opportunity to hold a clipboard or laptop and look as if you know what you are doing.

However, for someone who 'does Reiki' on whatever level, there is just you and this can feel very exposing, particularly when you are starting out. That can be why, even in those early days when you have recently completed your First Degree Reiki course (well done!) and will only be providing Reiki for friends and family, it can still be very helpful to invest in some Reiki equipment. If you have gained your Second Degree Reiki certification (brilliant!) and intend to work with members of the public, then having the appropriate items will be an essential step. Either way having access to the following will enable you to both look and feel professional in your new role, as well as helping every treatment you provide to go smoothly.

Therapy Couch

If working with friends and family, it is perfectly acceptable to work with the recipient sitting on a hard-backed chair. You might believe the better option would be on a sofa, bed, or comfy chair, but there will be both height and access issues with these. Even if you don't have any back or flexibility issues yourself, I promise you that ten minutes into the treatment you'll become aware of how restrictive they can be. It's good to know therefore that a hard chair is a perfectly good option, and one that is used even within the professional workplace, such as for those who lack the mobility to manoeuvre onto any sort of massage table. You will not, therefore, be providing a sub-standard treatment.

Investment in a therapy couch is however the optimum choice, and naturally a requirement as soon as you intend to begin working with clients. When I started out, I purchased the best massage table that I felt I could afford, only to find out a few months later, that a style designated specifically as a 'Reiki Couch' existed. It left me worrying about whether I had just invested in completely the wrong thing.

Well yes, actually I had, but that was really only because it weighed a ton and was far too cumbersome for a woman with zero upper body strength to hulk around with her in and out of cars and up and down flights of steps.

Several months later still, I established that a couch created with our style of therapy in mind is simply one that allows for you to sit down at the head end with your knees comfortably underneath it, whilst those designed for massage often have a board across the end which makes this impossible. You can therefore work with either. Stress over.

Do, however, consider the weight issue if you are intending to travel with your therapy bed. If you are buying from the Internet, read up on the number of kilogrammes you will be lugging about with you. Try lifting something of similar mass that you already possess and imagine carting it around for a good dose of practicality over ideal style or colour. There will be a balance between getting yourself a sturdy option, which can support larger individuals (weight and length) and movability.

My beautifully padded heavy-duty couch was substituted for a much lighter version as soon as my head could justify another round of expenditure.

Consider also whether your mode of transport can accommodate its size. And with hindsight, even storage is something that would have steered me in a different direction. The initial couch was too big to go anywhere other than a spare room. The second version fits in the back of a wardrobe. Lovely.

And don't imagine that a carry case is necessarily helpful. Having bought one, I found that the over-shoulder strap kept slipping down off my shoulders and actually it was much easier to hold the couch by its own handle. The case's side pocket that had seemed oh-so-handy for putting many undecided things in at the time of purchase, meant that when anything was put in it, the bed would no longer balance in an upright position but would promptly fall over at every opportunity.

To cover instances where you work with someone lying face downwards, you will need either a face-hole aperture or a couch that comes with a face cradle (an add-on attachment).

If you are tall in stature, make sure that the legs are height-adjustable to a level comfortable for you to work at. This may also mean you require a stepping stool for your more petite clients. Make sure said stool is made for adults and is sturdy enough to accommodate any of your heavier clients. My first one, which on reflection was perhaps more designed for a child to sit on, broke as a client stepped upon it. Her foot literally went right through the middle of it. I was mortified.

Be prepared for people of all shapes and sizes to come your way.

Covers, Towels & Blankets

Couch covers vary in size. They need to match your requirements so do make sure the length and width of any you purchase is clearly stated.

When swapping to my second purchase of the light-weight bed, I hadn't taken into consideration that it was also going to be narrower. The covers I owned were therefore no longer pristine tight and unable to provide the smooth foundation that I was aiming for. If you are upgrading to a wider bed please note that your old covers may not fit at all.

Improvising with some ironing-board-cover straps solved my issue by allowing me to tighten my existing covers from the underside of the therapy couch. But clearly it is worthwhile reviewing both the width and also the way in which a cover is affixed – elastic, drawstring etc. – before purchase.

Some covers will have a face-hole, others not. Naturally, if your table does, so should your cover.

Wanting the best for your clients and their experiences with you doesn't mean spending beyond your means. The value of yourself and the Reiki you channel is by far the over-riding factor. Although it is lovely to work with good quality towels for instance, clients will be fully clothed for a treatment so do feel comfortable sticking to an appropriate budget. For reasons of hygiene you will need to place towels over your couch cover and pillows. Or you may decide to use paper couch roll, sometimes referred to as massage paper roll, which will save on the laundry and mean you won't need a stock of clean towels if you have more than one client in a day.

Either way, you will also need to provide a blanket to place over your recipients. This will keep their muscles warm so that it is easier for them to relax. A person's body can cool more quickly than you might think when lying still for an hour. That said, it's always best to ask if someone would like to accept a cover, as in my experience a significant proportion of men and the occasional woman (especially if menopausal) will decline.

It is worthwhile making your clients understand they can change their mind in either direction part-way through a treatment, because the Reiki itself may affect their body temperature sufficiently to create the need. Although the majority of my clients feel Reiki as heat, there are those that sense it as coolness and an occasional person will find it makes them cold. Both can be true simultaneously too – I had one client who told me that the complete right side of his body went warm whilst the left side cold during a session. Reiki never ceases to remind us how individual we all are.

Wash-ability is something to consider.

Pillows

Someone lying on their stomach may require just one under their ankles. Someone lying on their back may require five. The record for one of my clients is nine, and I bet that has got you wondering how on earth that could possibly be the case.

Well, at my current venue, the pillows are particularly flat so the trend is definitely for more adventurous stacking than might usually be the case. Accordingly I can advise that you are likely to require fewer than half of my totals. So before you denude Dunelm of its pillow aisle, know that if you are using a standard depth of filling then two to three will almost always suffice.

With the stuffing knocked out of mine, generally I'll have three under a person's head. I place two under their knees, to provide support to their back if they are lying in the traditional way with their face upwards. If someone wishes to lie on their side – particularly common in pregnancy – then do offer them a pillow to place between their knees. It's often gratefully received. And for those who choose to lie on their front, as mentioned, it is advisable to offer one for under their ankles.

The story of the nine is perfectly true but very unusual. The client concerned had recently shattered her heel and had her foot and lower leg encased in a supportive medical 'boot' from the hospital. Having been instructed to keep her leg elevated, she needed a series of layered cushions starting from underneath the top of her legs down to her feet, and then because her leg kept rolling off to one side, further cushion scaffolding to hold it in place.

It's not only Scouts who should stand by the motto "*be prepared.*"

Music (Please also see Music (Public Performance) Licenses on page 89)

The practice sessions on my Reiki training were always accompanied by background music. It seemed only natural therefore to continue in that vein. We're talking many years ago now and CDs were the norm. So before I started giving my own Reiki treatments, I ventured to a local shop to purchase something suitable.

There on the shelf was a CD made specifically for Reiki. Gosh, *Reiki music*. Got to be better than general music or any designed with other methodologies in mind, hasn't it?

That's the thing when you're starting out and feel you've got to get everything 'right', you can think that anything else just might fall into a 'wrong' category.

CD purchased, played and regretted. If I use the term "plink-y plonk" does it conjure up a style for you? It just really wasn't a good choice for *me*. Maybe perfect for many others, but it didn't represent who I am. I stuck with it for quite a while though, whilst my self-doubt pondered on the efficacy of choosing something that wasn't seemingly 'correct' for my particular style of therapy.

After a while, it got on my nerves so much that I purchased a few other options and calmness was resumed. Now if I was getting irritated by my own choice of music, just think how annoying it can be to force your choice on someone else. Music can be a wonderful enhancer or it can grate so much that a treatment can be spoilt by it.

Ah ha. Time to think of how to offer *choice* to my clients.

Initial thoughts led me to offering each client the range of CDs I had at my disposal and asking them to select one, on the basis that if the cover artwork should be considered in breach of the Trade Descriptions Act, then we could always change to another at any point.

It took a specific client who had hearing problems to prompt me into additionally offering the option of peace and quiet. And there have been many times since when this has been readily accepted by my recipients, particularly, as it happens, musicians. Maybe they secretly don't think anyone should be playing something they haven't sanctioned themselves? No, I don't believe that either, but I would like you to benefit from knowing the possibility of silence can be a wonderful alternative for many people. After all, how often do we ever give ourselves that luxury?

On the other hand, most of my clients do select music and many comment that it helps their mind to settle down and be quieter as a consequence. Take note because it is therefore particularly worth considering in relation to clients who have a tendency towards anxiety. Moreover I will arrange to repeat play the same tracks on subsequent visits for such clients, so as to build an association between the music and calmer feelings.

Some albums designed for treatments, such as my original 'Reiki' CD, are divided into twelve tracks, with a view to denoting when to change hand positions. Whilst I have no structured hand positions to move to, because the type of Reiki I was instructed in was very 'free form' and intuition-led, I still noticed that if I changed position as a track finished, it was a harsh break. If the music has stopped and you've moved or maybe lifted your hands at the same time, it is more likely that your client is going to wonder if the treatment has finished (even if it is only a momentary question), and could therefore abruptly bring the recipient out of a deeply relaxed state. Waiting for the next track to begin and *then* moving I believe has offered more continuity and benefited my clients accordingly.

Remembering to place or remove your hands only very gently on the client's body, will also help maintain maximum relaxation. And if you are generally a little heavy handed as a rule, imagine you could almost slide a piece of tissue paper under your hands once they are in place. It will help you to keep them light.

And before we leave the subject, a quick (and probably unnecessary) reminder that, particularly if you are to travel to other people's homes as part of the service you offer, you will have to think through how you will play your music e.g. will you require an energy supply?

My current place of work has electrical sockets in the room. My mobile phone now supplies the tracks, and I have a small, lightweight Bluetooth speaker, which has enough power to see me through a clinic day. However in times past, I have worked with ageing phones, housing weakened batteries that require re-charging during my working hours. As well as unfamiliar rooms that mysteriously appear to be without an electrical socket, causing a momentary panic, whilst a brand new docking station has looked instantly obsolete.

There can be more than one reason to offer peace and quiet.

Clock

It's important to be able to time a treatment. Yet if your work takes you to other people's houses or venues, you can't always be sure there will be access to a clock.

As we move away from wristwatches and towards mobile phones, it's worth recognising there can be a few restrictions with the latter, including the fact that you can't just look up and see the time, you've got to actually tap a button to do so. This means you may have to break connection with your client and that's not a good choice to have to make.

Fleetingly I thought that I could just play music that lasted approximately sixty minutes and use that as a guideline. But what about when you start the music whilst you await your client's arrival and forget to re-set it? What about when you have had a long and detailed consultation with someone and you want (with their agreement) to give them more than the officially remaining thirty minutes of Reiki?

What happens when your client says they need to leave five minutes early to pick up their children? Or when you won't be playing any music at all? Also there are occasions when I want the Reiki to do its thing, but leave sufficient time near the end to supplement it with a visual releasing exercise. *"Oh good, eleven minutes left, perfect to start that now…"* Such instances require a clock.

Naturally, what type is a personal choice. But be aware that certain clients are so sensitive to sound they can find it distracting to hear the tick of a clock, because it focuses their attention on something external, making it harder to bring their awareness inwards. Accordingly it's worth considering going digital or using a timepiece that doesn't have a second hand movement.

And whilst we are considering issues around time, I think it only fair to let your client know when a treatment has come to an end. Having received a session from a therapist whose technique was to simply move away, I was left wondering *"what on earth should I be doing – has she finished? Is this just a long gap between elements of the healing, or is it over? Am I supposed to get up now or what?"* I am certain that from the perspective of the Practitioner, she was affording me the luxury of coming round in my own time. But actually it just left me questioning myself and feeling a little foolish, rather putting a dampener to the end of what had been a beautiful treatment.

My advice is to give people permission to take their own time to bring themselves back via a clear instruction to do so. I tend to use a softly spoken phrase such as, *"and now it's time to begin bringing all your energy and awareness fully back into the here and now. Have a gentle stretch of fingers and toes and when **you** feel ready, gently open your eyes and see how good you feel"* whilst gently touching their shoulder.

Thermometer

If you need to buy a clock as part of your treatment kit and you're going digital, consider buying one that includes a thermometer.

My hands under usual circumstances, are operating somewhere between a 'chilly' and an 'arctic' setting. (So are my feet but only my husband needs to be aware of that.) That is until I do Reiki. Then they take a quick holiday to the Sahara and often take the rest of my body with them. It means that I can lose all sense of whether a room is at a reasonable temperature, or not.

I can be working in the lightest of summer wear, though I may have arrived in jumper, fleece and winter coat. My client, on the other hand, may still be cold from their journey and then I'm asking them to lie down, relatively still, for almost an hour.

Employing a digital thermometer ensures the room remains at a pleasant temperature. It also counteracts any misunderstandings where a client feels coolness as a result of the Reiki energy changes. I've had a couple of people express they felt a bit cold during a treatment, with the implication being that they were being short-changed on the heating. It's great when you can point out that it is actually twenty two degrees, so their coolness is a sign that the Reiki is working well for them.

Out of interest it's worth mentioning again that the same client can be affected by the temperature of the energy in different ways simultaneously. For instance, although the majority of my clients appear to sense either heat *or* coolness during a treatment, particularly in the area where my hands are placed at the time, someone might feel say intense heat at their head but as if there were a cold breeze blowing across their stomach. Well, that's Reiki for you!

Water

Be sure to provide water to every client. Consider encouraging them to have some before you start the Reiki and certainly afterwards and for the rest of the day.

It is typical for people to notice they have a dry mouth after a treatment. I believe that this is the body unconsciously encouraging us to drink in order to assist it in cleansing itself. It's one of those wonderful ways in which our body talks to us and shows us how we can help it.

(Be mindful however never to over-ride a client's hydration advice from their General Practitioner (GP).)

Tissues

People may begin to cry as they describe their current circumstances or past traumas and, (as we'll note shortly) they may also do so during the treatment itself. There are many times when I've been grateful for having a box of tissues on stand-by and would recommend you keep some close-to-hand during your appointments.

Ear Plugs

You may encounter clients who are particularly susceptible to noise. Whilst for most, the Reiki is enough to lead them to a bubble of calm despite any external sounds, the occasional person demands a near-impossible silence. Now I like to point out in such instances, that the world we live in is rarely ever quiet (even nature is full of sound), and so there are benefits in using the Reiki treatment to begin to learn to 'switch off' in the midst of the distractions of daily life. In fact I highlight it as a much desired skill – to be aware of activity around them but nevertheless connect with their inner peace and calm. That's partly why they're here, right?

That said, if you are say unfortunate enough to have scheduled an appointment for the very time a nearby road is being dug up, then you may like to consider having some disposable mouldable silicone ear plugs to offer – naturally a pair should only be used once and then thrown away, so as to ensure you maintain scrupulous levels of hygiene.

Your Consultation Seating

It's important to meet your client on their level. By the end of an appointment, naturally we'll have hoped to have changed the way they feel in a positive direction, but initially we're looking to create a good and strong connection with the individual concerned. Whilst the Reiki energy will be working at numerous levels - beautifully doing its thing to change their energy - it's a good idea to ensure that physically we hear what our client has to say as an equal, so that we avoid coming across as superior in any way.

A simple way of achieving this, is to ensure that you both sit on similar (ideally the same) height of chair during the consultation, thereby maintaining eye contact without them either looking down or up to you. It's a simple thing but it really helps.

The Not To Have Things

Bad breath would be right up there, wouldn't it? Now I'm guessing that you don't generally fall into that category at all, but the chances are that you will one day eat garlic at lunchtime without any second thought for the fact that at 4:30pm you have a Reiki appointment. If you are working away from home, then a toothbrush and toothpaste can be a good addition to your Reiki 'kit'.

Likewise, I imagine that your choice is impeccable, so why would I remind you that it is worth avoiding perfume on a work day? Well simply because smell is an exceedingly personal thing and what attracts one person can repel another. More importantly some people are very sensitive to chemicals of any kind and whether it is perfume, incense or even candles they have the potential to provoke an allergic reaction.

Allergies also require consideration with regard to pets and pet hair. If you work from home and have pets, you would need to raise this with a client at the time of booking. If you have pets and don't work from home, you will still need to ensure that your blankets, towels, couch covers and so on, remain free from any animal hair or fur.

It's also worth avoiding loose clothing when you are due to work with someone because as you lean over their body, it may touch their skin and become a distraction. If you are a woman, then you may like to consider if a lower-cut top that looks beautiful when you're in an upright position, becomes less appropriate at another angle! Jewelry that jangles when you move can be an unwelcome distraction too.

First Degree Reiki (Level One)

Now I said I would tell you something of my own story, to impress upon those of you who struggle with feeling able to 'do Reiki' at all – those for whom an equipment list seems a long way off – to avoid giving up and talking yourself into believing it is not for you.

My working career began in the Civil Service and ended working for Reuters in The City of London. There was nothing in my childhood that gave me any cause to consider that something such as Reiki even existed, let alone that I would ever be drawn to it and love it as fully and completely as I do.

So when I began my training early in 2005 it surprised me as much as anyone who knew me. I had no history of complementary therapy. I had no friends working in this field, and nothing that was likely to attract me to it, except when a highly worrying and stressful health issue reared its ugly head and made me…panic!

Towards the end of 2003 I had been noticing how my fingers had been attracting more of my attention than usual. How I had somehow become increasingly aware and focused towards them. And then I started to feel pain and discomfort and noticed how they were beginning to become misshapen and distorted, protruding at the joints.

I was mostly comforted by a complete state of denial for a few months, until an awakening at 2:00am in the morning, in bed, next to my husband, when I suddenly felt the utmost terror and alarm. Not only did I, at this specific point, decide I did have a health issue, and one that needed to be addressed, I also had, in that very moment, decided that I needed to take *immediate* action.

What on earth had I been thinking of for all those weeks? Why hadn't I taken this seriously? What if I saw a doctor and he told me that if I had only come when I had first noticed it, that there would have been some miraculous cure, but now I'd left it to mid-December, there was absolutely nothing they could do? In fact it would have given them a fighting chance if I had come in before yesterday afternoon, but now... Aarrgghh. All I could do was load more guilt and anguish on to myself.

If there had been an emergency room in the small village in which I lived, I would have been down there in my dressing gown, banging on the door, but all I could do was wait.

First thing in the morning, I phoned the doctors. There was a five day wait for an appointment – an emergency appointment is apparently not available for a condition you have been avoiding for ages.

But then having decided to take action, waiting around for a doctor felt too much like continued inertia, and so I needed to look for other ways in which to do *something*. And so it is that I found myself reaching out to complementary healthcare, as a salve to my guilt-ridden wounds of previous inactivity.

In intense situations, more is definitely more, right? So I made not just one, but two appointments for the next two consecutive days.

One for acupuncture – weird that. I have a great fear of needles and yet I was drawn to lay out my whole body like a pin cushion. I can only think that the guilt of no activity was making me take to self-martyrdom.

Well wouldn't it be lovely if I said the other appointment was for Reiki? If I told you it worked like a dream and I became a therapist just as soon as I possible could?

But I can't, because actually it was Reflexology that spoke to me, and then my Reflexologist who literally spoke to me, and that is where it all started.

During my on-going treatments we would talk, and most of the conversation related to esoteric and spiritual matters.

[As a quick aside here, I would like to raise how hard it is, to find terms of expression which are not loaded in some way. Each of us will have a reaction based on our life experiences that will allow us to either embrace, remain neutral towards, or positively spit out like some foul tasting food (celery instantly comes to mind,) just a simple word or phrase. I struggle to find a term that expresses what I want to say better than using 'spiritual'.

What is it that conveys that part of us that is infinite and forever, that can support us through the experience of being human, should we choose to acknowledge it and request its assistance; that essence that is pure love, stretching across dimensions; our true spirit including, yet also beyond, the physical; that which can also simply express our living with love and kindness to ourselves and others? I don't know, so

I'm going to use 'spirituality' as my term of choice here. But please mentally replace it with whatever wording makes your heart sing, provides you with a lovingly supportive yet openly freeing expression of *you* and *all* that *you* are, and ultimately leads you to seeking and experiencing deeper levels of love.]

My Reflexologist was a brilliantly skilful therapist whom I nearly never met. When I arranged my first session with her, I was asked for the exact date and time of my birth. Not my date of birth you understand, but did I know the hour, the minutes and the location?

In those days I was far shyer and found it much harder to stand up for myself. So having been the one to instigate the phone call, I felt I had to follow-through with the appointment, despite huge reservations and nagging doubts that I was going too far off-piste with anything that wanted to make a connection between astrology and my health. So it was with great trepidation that I went to see…

…A wonderful and lovely woman named Brenda. She became a shining light in my life, as she guided the healing of my fingers, and opened my awareness to my spiritual self. As we talked, she mentioned on a few occasions how my energy was leading her to believe that I should become a 'healer' of some sort.

Her natural inclination was to guide me in the direction of becoming a fellow Reflexologist. I knew that I was never going to be a 'foot' person however, so I needed to look in a different direction.

Brenda brought my attention to the fact that the owner of the therapy rooms from which she was working, was a

Reiki Teacher, and that I might be interested in that line of therapy. And so I was introduced to David.

In order to decide whether I would have any interest in Reiki, I decided to attend a discussion group that David ran twice a month. It explored the esoteric side of life, a world away from my conventional up-bringing. This was investigating life from a less physical perspective, by reading the *energy* of this world in which we find ourselves. I was instantly hooked.

We debated the life lessons we felt we were trying to teach ourselves via the experiences of our day-to-day living. We encouraged each other to see the subtle signs and symbols that guide and direct life if you choose to look for them. Consequently we discussed synchronicities and viewed the events of each other's lives through a filter of both Soul and personality learning. We contemplated meta-physics, psychic phenomena, channelling – anything that might be weird to most people. It fascinated us and entranced me.

It had taken me all of about five minutes to decide to put my name down for David's next course a few months later. I was excited. Here I was going to study something that I really wanted to learn, not something I should or had to learn, not something that was from a text book. No. Here was the concept of fun and learning combined. It was one hundred and eighty degrees away from all the education I had ever experienced in my past.

I wanted to do it.

The combination of feeling I had a head start on now understanding something about energy, coupled with a passion for doing so, made me think that my training was going to be an easy delight from start to finish.

Oh dear. You just never stop learning do you?

My First Degree training was to take place over a weekend in January 2005. The venue (at David's therapy centre) meant that the tables and chairs I associated with education, were nowhere to be seen. Massive colourful floor cushions, in a comforting circle, were to be the seats of our learning.

I'd taken a note book. Well of course. I had written copious notes on every course I had ever been on. (Lack of self-trust to remember the facts, and a driver to the perfectionism that I felt I always needed to seek in myself.)

Then something weird happened. There wasn't really anything to take notes about. And yet I was being filled with knowledge and learning, as if I was in a beautiful conversation. Some people are just born to teach.

I was on my way to receiving a great shock though. I had felt a great and overly excitable longing to go on the course, even though I wasn't entirely sure what it was that I was going to learn. My expectations to be able to do whatever was asked of us, were pretty high, since David had made me feel I would take to Reiki easily, and of course Brenda had been telling me for months that I would make a good 'healer'. You can therefore imagine my surprise when we were instructed to break into pairs to practice Reiki on each other, and I felt, well…nothing.

Still in my mind's eye I can vividly recall images of me standing beside a therapy couch, my hands hovering in the air above a fellow pupil. Moving my hands up and down the recipient, waiting to feel the flow of Reiki energy. Frankly, however, it felt more as if I was acting out a weak mime of doing the ironing.

Shame and embarrassment were my over-riding emotions, as our teacher came into the room to see how we were getting on. Only to look at me rather incredulously, as he could feel the complete lack of energy emanating from anywhere in my body.

Was I trying too hard? Was it Reiki reflecting back at me my own self-doubt which has cursed my life these last fifty years or more? Were there blockages in my energy that needed to clear first, before I would be able to sense the flow? Looking back now, there was probably a degree of truth in all of those answers. My difficulty at the time, however, was that whilst my teacher was proclaiming that it is a natural right for anyone to engage with this energy and therefore to learn Reiki, it seemed to be beyond my reach. I simply couldn't fathom how on earth someone as keen as I was, could be finding it so incredibly difficult to sense.

Thanks to David's teaching skills everyone else on the course appeared to be connecting with great ease. I could feel differences as we swapped partners – amazing new sensations in my body. Sometimes more strongly than others, but always there nonetheless. Except when it came to me. I felt as if I was broken. But I also knew that if what David was telling us was correct – that anyone can learn Reiki – then this had to be a temporary situation.

Indeed, so many years later, I absolutely know this to be the case. If you are someone who is unable to sense it right now, then you simply need to regularly practise and it will come (more on this later).

Even if it does come easily to you, you may notice how many of your clients are surprised to be told that Reiki is available to all. Often their expectation is that there are a few special people who can connect to this powerful energy, and that they are somehow not special enough to do so. I trust you will know differently and can empower your clients accordingly.

Let me repeat, ***everyone can learn Reiki***, and in the clichéd words of many before me, *if I can do it then so can absolutely anyone*. I wonder now whether the very fact that I found it hard to begin with was a gift in order for me to help others to believe in their own latent abilities. But back then it was simply a reason to feel inadequate.

What's more, it appeared to be giving me an unanswerable conundrum – if you can't sense it, how on earth do you begin to do so?

If you are learning almost any other skill, you will have some concept of, or perhaps an ability to see, what it is you should be doing. Most likely you will be able to feel the tools of your trade – whether it's a computer keyboard or a cashier's till – even if you don't yet know how to use them. Goodness, when you learn to cook, you can at least both feel and see the ingredients, even if your end result looks nothing like the beautiful picture in the recipe book.

In most scenarios you will have a *thing*, whether that thing is as big as a tangible product, or as little as a set of numbers to work with. But an energy that you can't see or feel – how do you get *there*? Particularly as none of my fellow pupils appeared to be experiencing similar difficulties.

I was on a course with a mixed set of six people, including someone who was a Pilates teacher. When it came to introducing ourselves, at the beginning of the first day, she had recounted that in doing her job, as she helped move members of her class into the correct positions, certain students had been asking her what it was that flowed through her and into them? Apparently they could feel a type of supportive and loving energy emanating from her. She had no idea what it was. Investigation had led her to understand that it was Reiki, which was why she had booked herself on the course.

How unfair. How unjust. How is it that someone who isn't seeking it can find it and yet I, having even paid for the privilege, was completely unable to gain the merest whiff of it?

This is Reiki.

Part of Reiki's gift is to remove competitiveness. We should never be looking at how well we are doing compared to others. Our barometer for advancement is how far we have personally come, and what understandings are relevant to us as individuals.

It is why I believe that you will always get the clients that are right for you. You can have a healing centre or town full of Reiki therapists, and not one of them will ever be able to 'take' your clients. You offer a specific vibration of your own, and the appropriate people will be attracted to it.

You will always receive the right clients as reflected by your own energy. Don't look to others as being either better or worse than yourself, just different. And in that difference, the matching of therapist with recipient will sometimes happen for reasons beyond our limited awareness.

And of course there is no Reiki-ometer available. We cannot plug ourselves into a machine and have our Reiki delivery evaluated in comparison with others. So Reiki requires trust, not least because we can never know exactly what any recipient will be feeling.

In fact there have been countless times when I have had someone offer a very meagre response back to my request for post-treatment feedback – *"oh I feel much more relaxed now thank you"* – and I've allowed myself to feel rather deflated as a consequence. Only to find when they return maybe six months later, that they make a throw away comment such as *"because last time I came here it was absolutely amazing. I have never felt anything like it, it blew me away."*

You mean I did a really good job and had been left with the merest faint praise???

Reiki asks you to value yourself, for yourself, not because of what others say.

Accordingly we need to focus on our relationship with ourselves. Finding our own self-worth, rather than depending on others to create it. We also need to view the achievements of others as inspiration rather than competition.

Reiki will take you on a journey of deep self-awareness if you let it.

After that initial First Degree course, Reiki was speaking to me at a deeper level than my logical mind. Because traditionally I would have tended to have given up at this early stage having felt I had no great potential or ability for success.

So I guess it must have been having a conversation with my heart. Because here I was being fascinated by the very idea of it. Finding the desire to learn to 'do it' was far more compelling than the embarrassment that I couldn't. A new Sarah was emerging.

This is where I surprised myself. If I was to train to Second Degree level, then I had to find some way to improve. Somehow I had to learn to do what I felt I couldn't learn. All the others on my course, naturally and effortlessly, connecting and channelling the energy. How could I make myself 'work'?

It's the problem with something so nebulous, particularly as the type of Reiki I was instructed in didn't require the rituals and guidelines that are an integral part of some methods of learning this form of therapy. Here there were no specific hand positions. No order in which to work up or down the body. David asked us to be guided by our intuition alone.

How very healing in itself, for someone whose previous learning had always been very structured. All academic. All very exact. In the past I had been able to take verbatim notes on what the teacher was teaching. How very Reiki that I should come to learn it in the exact opposite way.

Which reminds me how the other day I was talking to a friend who is thinking of embarking on Reiki Level One. She wanted to chat through what I felt she should consider when selecting the appropriate course for her. I felt obliged to say how important I feel it is to choose both the style and teacher on a very personal and individual basis. There is no right way to learn. No one style that is better than any other. You simply need to feel it's right for you. Hence what she would find was the right style for her might (just as it was for me), be the antithesis of what she would expect.

Reiki, after all, is a way of learning about yourself and bringing balance.

Does it surprise you to learn that there is more than one form of Reiki out there? In fact The Reiki Council website lists 13 different styles and those don't include options such as Angelic or Shamanic Reiki. And within each of these choices, there can be great variety of content, because in each instance it will also be dependent upon the specific beliefs of the teacher and their teacher before them.

Speak to the person running any course before you book with them. Match yourself as much as possible to the one that will ignite your passion. And if your choice fails to do so, then consider a complete change of teacher and/or method.

For someone like me who had always learnt everything in a very defined and restrictive style, I was astounded and delighted that my course was run without any tests or exams. There was no pressure to prove you were learning 'correctly'. Just information being shared.

Goodness. You mean you can learn something where there is only *your* way to do it? Where there isn't a right or wrong way? It seemed the very foundations of the way life works, were being re-formed at such a deep level, that it was making me question myself to the very core of my being.

I was learning freedom.

How Do You Do It?

If you want more of something, do it more. Even if a part of you is saying *"I don't know how."* Just do something that seems in some way to bring it closer to you.

Now that sounds so very obvious, that you may wonder why I have taken up your valuable time asking you to read it. However I have noticed that for me, and also many of my clients, it is often obvious common sense that is on offer in abundance in those areas of our life where we tend to handle things well. But it's overly elusive in those areas we are struggling with. With the former we wonder how on earth someone can find something we find easy, so difficult. And vice versa with the latter.

Where we don't feel that we know how to get it, do it, be it, common sense just doesn't seem to show up.

I felt I didn't know how to generate my connection to Reiki, I simply knew I really wanted to. To a certain extent, the 'do more of it' (common sense) didn't make sense to me. Because if you don't feel you are doing it when you are doing it, then doing more of it is actually just more of not doing it.

If when I started I had felt that I was 'doing Reiki' even if only a little, it would have been easier to convince myself to continue, and thereby improve. But initially that just wasn't happening for me.

So I'm going to labour the point. Because whilst I guess and indeed hope that 99% of you will be shouting out (like you do to the TV screen when a quiz show contestant can't answer a question) something along the lines of *"well just keep practising, keep intending, keep going,"* I want to help the other 1% that are feeling as I was. Those who really can't see how they can improve at something that appears to have to be given or sent to you, rather than acquired by personal effort.

But my heart wanted Reiki even more than my head, so something deep within me did say: *"keep trying even though you don't think that is helping much"*. But it was a small quiet voice which would have been easy to ignore. Nothing big and brash about it and very much in the background behind a load of thoughts of "how?" "when?" and "can I?"

Listen to your heart rather than your head for the really good advice. Eventually there will be a breakthrough, even if you can't imagine success.

Somehow I made myself continue rather than turn in another direction, and proved a little more courageous than I would have given myself credit for. My heart-felt intuition was chipping away at my self-doubt and feelings of inadequacy, by slowly encouraging me and leading me forward in small steps.

More than half of me was all for leaving things as they were, wanting to believe that I should simply attend the Reiki Level Two course in the hope that that would be the turning point. But fortunately, whatever fraction remained, brazenly went against what I would have considered was my better judgement, and pushed me to carry on taking action. And on two fronts.

Firstly the more understandable self-Reiki route. There's safety in trying it in your own home with only yourself for company. Secondly though, I took the momentous decision to carry out some treatments on other people. I know. Bravery I never knew I had.

The self-Reiki began as just resting my hands on my stomach, heart, chest, with intention. That was it. But let me encourage you to do the same. Because doing this regularly began to slowly and surely bring Reiki sensations similar to those that I had felt from my fellow pupils on my Level One course.

I hope that your training has covered self-treatment as fully as you would wish. However, the other day I met with someone who had recently completed her first level training and she still wanted to hear about it from my perspective. So with the thought that the following might augment what you have already been shown, let me say this.

You can do self-healing at any time - in a supermarket queue, watching TV etc. It's your life force energy so it's there all of the time and doesn't require particular circumstances. That said, when starting out it can be very helpful to set aside some quiet time to improve one's focus. Not least because the act of setting up a form of ritual (such as sitting in a particular place with a particular intention) allows our conscious mind to tell our unconscious that we are doing something important, and therefore engage our resources more fully. And when we are at the beginning of any new practice, we generally need to create the best environment for us to succeed. As we continue however, and the task we've set ourselves comes more naturally, we can then do it in almost any situation.

The position of the body doesn't matter. So if you want to sit, or if you choose to lie down, it is purely up to personal preference.

If it's difficult to find the time for self-Reiki, then think about allocating those moments in bed before you go to sleep. I tend to do this most nights anyway, no matter how much I have given myself Reiki during the day. And if you are a mother of young children, even setting aside a few minutes whilst you're sitting on the loo or lying in the bath, can make all the difference.

I used to set a clear mental intention before starting (e.g. *"I'm now going to use Reiki to help me heal myself"/"I'm now going to allow Reiki to help bring me back into balance"*).

Intention is always important.

Then I would place my hands gently on my body (usually at the heart, stomach and/or abdomen), so that my arms and shoulders felt relaxed, meaning my focus could be on gently comforting my body and my physical being. If you've been taught specific hand positions, just become aware whether using them leads to too much of your attention focusing on the discomfort of maintaining them exactly. You can always revert to them when the Reiki is flowing well for you, or employ them only when working on others.

You may have been taught Reiki as a non-touch experience, only as light touch, or a mixture of both methods. I found it easier to work with touch initially. Particularly for self-healing (though currently use both styles on myself and also when working with others – allowing my intuition to guide me). Resting my hands on my body felt as if it enhanced the feeling of connection and engendered a greater sense of self-care. I hoped that would translate into improving my chances of the Reiki flowing.

I would remind myself that Reiki is there to help me to re-balance the mind, the body and the emotions. Then gently move my mind-set to one of loving kindness; full of compassion – as if I were going to be giving Reiki to a baby. If you are able to create mind's eye images, then you might visualise pure light entering through your head (crown chakra), flowing down to your hands and that light then passing into your body. (That isn't quite how I sense it now but it was really helpful imagery in the beginning.)

Avoid judging how you are doing based on how much you are feeling. It's very easy to do, but rather unhelpful. It's a delight when you feel definite feedback that it's working, when you can sense warmth, coolness, tingling, pressure, see colours etc. But with your intention clearly set, you will always be 'doing it right'; we're really just then talking about the degree of proficiency.

Reiki is a lot about building self-trust, so be gentle on yourself.

Really the only way to get over self-doubt is by doing, practising and repeating so that confidence begins to come. And whilst self-treatment has since been a welcome comfort in my everyday life, I know that back then it was critical in opening up the channel of connection. I also believe that at the same time, The Universe was getting me to realise the value of commitment and self-discipline, neither of which feature highly in me by natural inclination.

In fact Reiki, it seemed, had become a bit of a must-have. Usually I am the person who has the dedication of an

Olympic spectator (turn up on the day, for a few hours every four years), rather than an Olympic athlete. Yet here I was showing a degree of dedication.

It amazed me that I persevered enough to result in tentative responses, which could only confirm it was working. Gentle and fleeting sensations, such as warmth or tingling, when I placed my hands on my body with intention. And the feeling of a pull of energy through my hands as I did so.

Wow, maybe I can do Reiki after all. Maybe there is hope for me yet.

More than a decade later I can now initiate a Reiki session in myself at the merest thought of it. I can be watching TV, just think how beneficial some Reiki would be and it can be as if I had taken myself to a fellow Practitioner. You can be sure that slowly, stronger and more broad-ranging feelings come – I promise you it builds.

Remember that I started at zero and let me encourage you that whether 'doing Reiki' is the *"how on earth do I get to do what I want to do?"* question for you, or whether it arises in any another aspect of your life, simply keep taking the small steps that you *sense* might bring you closer to what you seek. You never know when you'll reach your tipping point. Keep faith in yourself; you're worth it.

Back then though, I was under pressure since there was only a small amount of time until to my next course. The Second Degree (Reiki Level Two) training was scheduled for the month of May. This meant I was also going to have to 'do it for real' and soon. What's more, doing it was going to have to involve someone else, which might only provide an opportunity for me to prove how elusive it was being. The potential for failure witnessed by another, was a hard option to contemplate.

Additionally at that time I didn't know anyone 'in the trade' so to speak. So there wasn't going to be someone in the Reiki world that could help guide and reassure me. This meant that I was going to have to be at my bravest and ask to give Reiki to someone who was probably at best a sceptic and simply trying to be helpful to me. This was heart-pounding scary. This was putting myself on the line.

But there was nothing else for it. No way other than to face it head on. Somehow I felt compelled to come out of my comfort zone and go against my usual instincts. So I offered my services where I thought it appropriate, and to people whom I felt would be as supportive as they could without being false. I only wanted true feedback and certainly didn't want people to tell me what I would most like to hear but without the foundation of truth. And that meant going the hard way, by not using close friends who might try and bolster my ego. I needed someone that would have less investment in protecting my vulnerability.

Thankfully I found that someone in a member of my badminton club, who was kind enough to have let me 'have a go' and fitted the bill perfectly, since we only ever met on court.

Knowing that I wanted to look as professional as possible, meant some investment in a therapy couch, cover, blanket and some pillows which I duly obtained.

Then came the heart-pounding moment when I had to knock on her front door. Therapy couch lugged up her drive and questions such as *"did I check that the legs are set at a comfortable working height"* wafting in and out of my brain, in between my shallow breaths. It would have been a great time for some deep breathing, but I was a few years away from being aware of that technique. I was going in rookie style.

Erecting the couch – question: *"Do you ask for help to make it effortless, or do the professional thing and handle it all yourself, but realise that you should have had a bit of a practice first?"* Couch up. Pillows on. Remember one under the knees to support the back – ah a bit of professionalism there Sarah, well done.

Now, a bit of explanation of what Reiki is and how it might feel. Panic. Not really sure how to explain Reiki. All seemed very clear before but now just flustered by thoughts of how do you explain the inexplicable? I'm sure I was just going to say a few key phrases, so how come I can't think of a single one of them now?

Goodness, I was so nervous that I thought my hands would tremble to such a degree that she might think it was an essential part of the treatment! But I wanted to work with light touch because in my head that would make it easier for her to 'feel' the Reiki. Touch was how I was working on myself when I felt it, so it was too much of a risk to hold my hands above her body.

You can imagine the enormous relief I felt when at the end of the first treatment she confirmed that she had been able to notice a range of strange sensations. I can't now recall whether it was her arm or shoulder that had been giving her problems. But I do remember that she appeared to notice physical improvements in her body over the course of the three treatments I gave her. What's more I was *finally* feeling some energy flowing through me during the sessions too. My hands giving me some feedback that they really might be emitting that thing we call Reiki.

For any of you finding that the stress brought on by those first few 'clients' seems to place a brain freeze on your ability to explain what a treatment is or does, don't worry, this can be a common experience.

Whilst in the longer term you are likely to tailor your description according to the person sitting in front of you, in the short term it will generally work well to recite just a simple sentence or two. I have noticed how mentioning the 'spiritual' element of Reiki is *not* the best way forward, and can turn people off, or leave them confused or overwhelmed – unless they have specifically come with a spiritual purpose in mind. Generally it is best left for discussion after the treatment has taken place, if this is warranted.

To ensure a client feels both comfortable and safe, it is usually beneficial to concentrate on the less esoteric aspects. Have a practice finding the phrases you are most comfortable with. You may like to consider including something along the following lines: *Reiki is a way of releasing stress and bringing relaxation, which aids the body's natural ability to heal itself. Stress is acknowledged as a major factor in creating health conditions, and a Reiki Practitioner is trained to facilitate an individual's ability to bring their mind, body and emotions towards an inner state of balance and calm, allowing the release of stress. In the UK, Reiki is now available in traditional healthcare environments – such as hospitals – as the medical community endorse its use in clinical settings. Because it is non-invasive, and at most uses only very gentle light touch, it is entirely safe, as well as being a beautifully peaceful and calming therapy.*

Do also read the chapter dedicated to *The Consultation* which includes a lot more information on this subject.

Second Degree Reiki (Level Two)

So now I had some sense of what Reiki felt like. And felt better prepared, and in truth more worthy, to attend the next level in my training.

I had already booked to go on the next Second Degree Reiki course David was running that May anyway. Since despite any personal inadequacies in connecting to the energy, just learning about it and experiencing it from others was more than enough to create an interest that wasn't going to go away. So much so that feeling I was bottom of the class was surprisingly not going to put me off.

The good news was, however, that I was now 'doing 'it', at least in a small way, and that made everything more pleasurable still.

No it didn't, it made it an exhilarating whoosh of fantastically magical, mind-blowing wonderfulness.

How boring everyday life felt in comparison to this.

On that weekend my fellow pupils were feeling Reiki through me, whether I touched them or not. I could feel 'weird' sensations in myself and had experiences such as feeling like I was flying like a bird, or out in space as the Reiki flowed. How exciting is that? Things happening beyond my regular sight or logic but irrefutably happening. This was truly amazing. And all in the name of healing and love. Surely it can't get any better?

But actually it has, because it never ceases to amaze me. More than a decade later and I continue to be like a curious child about the whole experience. It still makes me go 'wow' on a regular basis, and will forever allow me to grow into it.

As part of Reiki Level Two we were taught some of the *symbols* that connect you to and increase the power of your healing. I remember feeling the wonderful privilege of being introduced to such a sacred part of Reiki tradition.

My teacher, however, was of the opinion that their power exists because of our belief about the symbols, rather than the symbols themselves. And now, as far as I can attest, working with or without symbols really just comes down to your personal choice. That's why Reiki is so loving.

Love embraces difference and is non-judgemental.

My teacher effectively taught us the symbols for us to do with as we chose. They were available to view as the key to unlock a sacred portion of the energy that would not be available to us otherwise. Or simply as a means of bringing your mind into a place that could accept your own worth and value, and that of the energy you delivered to others. So therefore not a fundamental necessity to the process at all.

I experimented with them – just in case they increased the quality of energy I could channel, since (as I imagine you will feel), I always want the utmost healing experience for my clients. However, attempting to incorporate them in client sessions once my training was complete, never really felt appropriate to me. Somehow, as I drew them, it always felt like I was taking myself out of the moment, and directing my energy to 'doing more' rather than simply 'being enough'. Trying to make something happen, rather than trusting that the energy knew what was needed in each circumstance. Using my mind to remember them, rather than going with the natural flow of that energy.

It wasn't long before I was unable to deny that I had had some success with Reiki without assistance from the symbols, and decided to venture forth without them. Initially thinking that possibly as I progressed, the symbols might act like a powerhouse to take me to the next level at some point in the future.

Nowadays though, I accept that they are not appropriate in my case. And perhaps, this is not as singular as I had thought. Because someone told me the other day, how they had been taught the first two levels of their Reiki training using symbols. Only to be told on their final level by the same teacher, that they are unnecessary. How (in the viewpoint of that teacher), they are a beautiful way of providing a methodology for learning to connect to Reiki energy, which once integrated, is no longer required.

At the end of the day, this is not a place of right or wrong, simply what is best in your practice. And I do remember how someone, whose opinion I value highly, did make a very good point. They said that if hundreds of thousands of people are putting their energy (by way of belief and deference) into a symbol, and that is happening continually over many years, in some real and tangible way, surely that is creating a true power for that symbol?

The important fact is therefore that both view-points are entirely valid, and equally so. Neither are provable beyond establishing our own truth towards them, and of course that can change. What we reject at one point in our lives, can be transformational with its acceptance at some point in the future.

Any particular aspects you've been taught, that begin to take on more significance in your own practice, will come down to your personal relationship with it. Which is why it is critical to choose to train in a style that appeals to both your personality and beliefs.

I am learning, as part of my enlightening journey, that often there is not a black or white answer. There are all the colours in the middle and that they are a beautiful place in which to reside.

Third Degree Reiki (Master Level)

So fired up was I after my Second Degree course, that it was only a few months later, in September 2005, I was taking my Master (Level Three) course.

This was going to set me on my way to healing *as a career*. Wow. Doing this for a living. That was such an amazing thought.

Previously if you had told me there was even a hint that I could ever do a job that I really loved, then it would have been so far out of my sphere of comprehension, that I think I would have thought of you as very nice but completely out of touch with reality. It had just never been on my radar. But here I was, about to embark on a level of training that would open the door to me doing just that. Yippee. *My reality* was changing.

It's that old cliché of doors opening when you previously hadn't noticed that the door even existed. Suddenly you are walking into a new world of possibilities.

The course was a mixture of developing our connections to the energy, together with some practical aspects that running our own business would demand us to consider.

Part of the course involved us giving a presentation. It was strange because there was all the fear and self-doubt and feeling small and … (I'll save the ink as I'm sure you get the picture), and yet these feelings were somehow counteracted by the passion and wonder surrounding the subject matter. It was like the anxiety was almost irrelevant. Still there in a heart-thumping way that standing up to speak in front of other people brings me, but also in the background because here I was talking about Reiki, to other people that loved it too.

David was very careful to ensure that he gave us the maximum belief in ourselves and our Reiki skills, and also our ability to attract clients. From a stance where our beliefs create our experience, despite David feeling that he had fewer clients for his own Reiki practice than he would wish for, he did not want to taint our ability to create a flourishing business for ourselves.

However, this leads me to discuss the fact that it is hard to generate an appointment-filled diary with Reiki clients alone. Having spoken to others in the same profession, it appears to be an all too common experience to find that there will often be a gap between the number of treatments you would aspire to, and those that are actually forthcoming.

Now it may well be that this perception is merely my own reality reflected back to me. And that Practitioners outside of my awareness have more requests for treatments than they can handle. As with David, I would not wish for my experience to restrict your own in any way. What I will suggest, however, is that when you are starting out, do so on a part-time basis initially.

Fortunately with this style of business, you can usually hire a therapy room to work in on an hourly basis. Or maybe you will choose to work from home. Either way will reduce your overheads. I would certainly suggest that you avoid any contract with a third party that commits you to a weekly or monthly fee whether you have clients or not. At least until you are assured that your business can support this.

Be aware that Reiki is a very personal choice of treatment and not for everybody. This has led many of my fellow Practitioners to diversify by offering additional forms of therapy, to increase their client base. And whilst I have had many clients tell me that they sing my praises to their friends and family, the number of appointments that this has generated is not as substantial as you might expect.

Where you live will play its part too. There is no avoiding the fact that if you are based in a rural part of the country, your ability to attract a full diary of client appointments is much less realistic.

There is also likely to be a limit to the number of treatments that you would feel content with providing on any one day. I tend to find four a comfortable maximum. When there has been more, the tendency is to find that my head is floating so much in a detached other-worldly space, that I do not feel that my verbal skills are as highly tuned as they might be. Additionally, as you'll be aware, you are a receiver of Reiki at the same time as providing it for another. I think there is a point where your body just goes, *"thank you I've had enough for now; it's been wonderful but I need some time to process the changes that have been taking place."*

My advice is therefore to allow your Reiki treatments to be an additional form of income when starting out, rather than expecting it to be your main source of earnings. Oh, and we'll discuss the thorny issue of being paid for Reiki a little later on.

But for now, I was a *Master* Reiki Practitioner. The only problem was that I didn't have feelings that corresponded to the title. Now if it had been "Done Reiki Level Three and Loves it Practitioner" then I could easily have worn the badge, but it wasn't and so I couldn't, and it took rather a long time for me to feel worthy of doing so.

And that defies some logic I can tell you, because after the completion of my Master level course, David asked if I would like to come and work at his therapy centre. Would I *like*? I couldn't think of anything better. Without any effort on my part, I was being offered an opportunity that would otherwise have been considered purely an aspiration. But emotions are unwieldy creatures that don't follow logic.

Not only had my new career effectively been given a fabulous seal of approval by way of the venue. But additionally (after having accepted with possibly unseemly rapidity), there had been an early major boost which *logically* should have meant that my self-doubt should not even have taken a back seat, but rather have got out the car and walked, whilst I drove off into a beautiful sunset of possibilities.

Because within a week or so of starting to officially work as a Reiki Practitioner, David had found he was unable to provide a treatment to one of his clients. He asked me to fill in for him. And it gets better, the appointment went really well. The client expressing that he had felt stronger energy changes with my healing over David's. I mean, just how much of a gift was that kind of experience?

Well actually, only a teeny weeny very temporary gift. Writing this is actually causing me a degree of anguish. Because it gives me cause to wonder how differently things might have turned out if I had been able to hear the praise and *fully accept* it. Oh I heard the words this client said.

And a little bit of me was doing a happy dance all the way home. I bathed in its joy for a whole evening of utter delight. Goodness, I might have started slowly but now I was on the fast track. Now I was blazing a trail.

But for it to stand as a new way of thinking about my Reiki skills, it would require that my mind was able to accept what my heart wanted to hear. Sadly it couldn't.

This beautiful moment was therefore downgraded to a momentary blip. A happy circumstance that merited but short celebration. Then back to the serious business of being seriously unsure of oneself. Yeah, that was where familiarity lay.

My comfort zone, as for many others, isn't really comfortable at all. Just a bad emotional habit that I accept as representing who and what I am. What's more, with my insistence that thinking too positively of my new-found skill, would be aligning too much with ego, I could fend off any pesky thoughts of ability for years to come.

Self-awareness can make us walk a thin tightrope. We know that we don't want to become big-headed in anyway but sometimes our avoidance in that direction takes us too far in the other. We use an argument that ensures we don't become a negative extreme, as a justification for maintaining an equally negative status quo.

Sometimes you have to ask yourself why on earth thinking that you are good at something, can be anything other than a good thing.

And maybe it has more to do with how much importance you place upon the thing in question? I mean, I know that I am good at making choux pastry. I treat it as a fact. A nice thing to be able to do. I don't imagine that being able to admit this ability, even in print, is going to make me manically egotistical.

There is no need for me to even mention it in my day-to-day life. Never have I pinned some poor unsuspecting newly found acquaintance against a wall, to ensure they knew that, if we were really up against it and life expectancy were reliant upon the production of a chocolate éclair, they could consider themselves in a safe pair of hands.

Which leads me to ask if our emotional frailty is generally exposed only in direct proportion to our desire? That we find fault with ourselves all too eagerly only in those arenas in which we care a great deal about our achievements?

If you incline towards a difficulty in receiving compliments – and particularly if you realise that you traditionally bat away praise as effectively as a service return in a Wimbledon tennis match – then how about agreeing now to see what it is like to simply accept it? Even if as nothing more than one person's totally valid view of you.

Then go further and contemplate if this could be an opinion that goes beyond one individual.

What if thinking you are not good enough is only in your head and isn't a true picture at all?

What does it *feel* like, even just to play with the feeling that they are able to see something in you that you fail to appreciate in yourself?

What if you are far more amazing than you have ever given yourself credit for?

Although I was tainting how I viewed myself, the one thing that couldn't be sullied was my feelings around Reiki itself. And I would love to share with you the sheer exuberance I felt then, and still feel now, when I provide a Reiki treatment. My fascination and pleasure has in no way diminished through the years.

When I introduce people to a world of sensations that they had no idea existed – when they begin to feel more love, peacefulness or joy through those magical vibrations – there is almost no better feeling in the world.

The unmatched beauty of leading someone into the realisation that neither the world, nor even their own body can be quite what it has formerly seemed to be, because they have now been awakened to never-before-felt sensations and levels of awareness. Wonderful. In fact, wonder full.

That feeling when you have seen someone walk in looking sorrowful and with the weight of the world on their shoulders, only to leave with a brightness and smile that tells you that you have lifted their spirits in a way their mind has yet to make sense of. Because there is little sweeter in my estimation than when someone gets up off the therapy couch and looks at you in wondrous curiosity. Marvelling that so much can have happened whilst being so inactive. It captures my heart; that shared moment when you've both felt the exquisite enchantment in the exchange of such beautiful energy.

And that happens by providing Reiki exactly as you will have practised it in your training. There is no need to do anything more than that in any treatment. It means, as soon as you have reached the stage where you know the energy is flowing through you, you can provide similar experiences for your clients. It doesn't mean you won't notice improvements as you continue in the role. But it does mean that you don't have to invite self-doubt in as company.

Please therefore, don't question whether you need to embellish your skills with additional techniques (such as using visualisations which I'll mention a little later on). They are not a sign of becoming a 'better' Practitioner. They potentially offer examples of how one can assist a client's mind to initiate or accept a change in their energy. But if you think you are not good enough when you don't employ them then STOP.

Realise that by doing Reiki the way you have been taught, you might just be doing the most powerful thing you can do to help someone. Because most times we really do need to just get ourselves *completely* out of the way. That trying to do more is counter-productive. And stepping aside and letting the innate intelligence both of the energy and of the recipient, do whatever they know is needed, is absolutely the best thing to do. No more, no less.

Signs It's Working

I raised the importance of recognising how you see yourself and value your abilities at the end of the last chapter, because it can have some bearing on how you feel as you work with Reiki energy.

When you have someone lying in your care receiving Reiki, most times they will have their eyes closed and there will be no verbal communication between you. Particularly when you are newly trained, it can be difficult not to let your critical inner voice begin to raise doubts about the quality of the treatment they are receiving, for no other reason than you are not getting any feedback.

With experience you'll realise that even when your 'client' (substitute 'friend' or 'family member' as appropriate) appears to be distracted because they keep rubbing their eye or nose, resting their head in one position and then another, or changing the position of their arms – folded across their abdomen, then along by their sides – it is still not necessarily telling you anything more than that they are moving. Indeed it may even be a sign that a great deal is going on for them, as it's possible that the person is moving their arms about because their fingers are feeling numb or getting pins and needles from the Reiki.

You never really know what is happening for anyone. So do keep positive. This can be made much easier, by focusing on what you are providing (such as the pull of the energy through your hands), rather than what you imagine they might be receiving.

If you aren't feeling the energy much yourself, then if you are working off the body try placing your hands on the body or vice versa. When working off the body and not sensing the energy greatly, try swaying your hands or circling them as the movement may enable you to feel variations more easily.

At some point you will begin to know and trust that your treatment is providing all that it can, no matter what the feedback. However in the meantime, it can be helpful to look for a few physical signs that will help you relax and silence the questioning "*is it working?*"

Likely indicators to show someone is responding to the energy include the following:

Breathing Changes

Notice the breathing pattern of your recipient and how it subtly changes during the session. You may see, hear, or feel the pattern of their breathing slow, or become more measured, as they relax into the treatment.

It can also be very satisfying to recognise a sharper intake (or alternatively a more defined release) of breath – it's not what would be happening if they were just lying down in a room on their own. Some change has forced that to happen.

Occasionally changes in breath become more obvious. Such as when a client begins to snore. This does not always mean that they are completely asleep, because they may well be drifting in and out of different levels of consciousness. So always continue to work as if they are fully alert. Instances where they have gone to sleep should be welcomed though, as this will tell you that they felt safe and trusting enough in your company to do so. Additionally it removes the logical mind from the healing, meaning the energy can work without restriction – a point of total surrender has been reached.

Less rare than you would imagine is a state of non-breath. (Don't worry, I've never lost a client yet!) I have had several recipients tell me that they felt they have moved into a state beyond the need for breathing.

I was first alerted to this as a possibility on one of my Reiki training courses. My teacher said that he had once witnessed a client who appeared to stop breathing completely. Thankfully the person was perfectly unaffected by experience, and came round at the end of the treatment as if nothing extraordinary had happened. I remember silently praying for no one on my therapy couch to ever go through this. And yet they have, and on more than a few occasions. Fortunately I can now appreciate that this phenomenon is just one of those beautiful mysteries that surround Reiki, or rather altered energy states, as I've heard it has also been observed occurring during deep meditation, so isn't specific to our form of therapy.

Stomach Gurgling

It is common for a person's stomach to gurgle. This is a very positive sign – where the digestive system is responding to energy changes. But unfortunately it is often coupled with a sense of shame. Most of us typically feel a sense of embarrassment when it happens, but please put your client at ease under such circumstances. When I have forgotten to mention up front that this is a regular experience, I softly say on the first time it happens, something like *"and welcome any energy movements in your stomach, as confirmation of your body responding well to the Reiki."*

Coughing

Bit of an odd one this, as it may of course be a 'normal' cough that's just a very minor disturbance, to an otherwise restful experience. However, be aware that sometimes coughing definitely is a way of clearing out energy from the body. Essentially it is another example of an unconscious, unrequested response. As such it's a sign of the body doing what it feels it needs to do. Physically reacting to the Reiki by forcefully expelling energy.

It can be very helpful to highlight to a client the potential benefit – that it's a form of 'letting go' in some way. Assuring them they do not need to apologise for the event.

Be aware though, that the one doing the coughing can, on occasion, be you.

It took me several years to establish that a particular type of cough takes me over, when it isn't (in a way) anything to do with me – when it's more about helping the client to release energy that they cannot. The reason it took so long was that I had to agree with myself that it wasn't just random coughing that was affecting me. I kept questioning *"Why do I need to cough just once or twice in that treatment, and at no other time in the last five months?"* Part of my answer came with the fact that this particular type of energy release causes my throat to constrict in a particularly unpleasant way first. This fact enabled me to assess that the cough was 'different' to what I would consider usual. I don't want to put you off. It is after all just a minor inconvenience. But my throat tightens like it's being twisted and compressed, and there is no way of suppressing it. It's coming out whether I want it to or not.

Having discussed the situation with other Practitioners, I realise I am not alone. Whilst infrequent, this means it is entirely possible that you could find it happening to you too. If you do, just go with it, and be pleased that whatever is going on is significant enough to cause such a strong physical reaction. It's worth noting too that when I shared the possibility of coughing with the lovely people who follow my Working with Reiki Facebook Page, a few of them mentioned how they sometimes experience an elongated yawn as an indication of significant energy changes taking place. As with the cough it can signal the cleaning of energy, or as a prefix to a deepening connection and all that that reveals.

Swallowing

Swallowing is an unconscious response and so when this increases or becomes noticeable it may show that the client is moving into a less conscious state.

Rapid Eye Movement and Blinking

Rapid Eye Movement (a person's eyes moving behind their closed eyelids) is generally associated with a specific level of consciousness within sleep. You are likely, however, to see this being experienced by your clients during a treatment. It is a great sign that some kind of processing is occurring. Blinking (with their eyes closed), also tends to happen when Reiki is working well. Brilliant.

By the way though, I had one client who had her eyes open during almost all of her session. In discussing the treatment afterwards, (whilst expecting her to have felt largely unaffected by the energy), she told me that she had felt like she was dreaming with her eyes open and that it had therefore been an incredibly other-worldly experience, the like of which she had never encountered before.

Everyone's beautifully unique in this world, remember that.

Movements of the Face or Body

Any unconscious movements from your client, are showing you that something is happening beyond their control – usually a sign that something very promising is taking place. It may lead you to notice twitching of their body in one area (e.g. a leg, fingers on one hand, a shoulder), or many. It is also common to notice facial twitches, such as eyebrows, forehead, or around the mouth.

In my opinion these small adjustments will be either re-aligning the body in some way, or they will represent an emotional release, where the body is letting go of past trauma or stress that has been embedded within it.

Be aware however, that the movements may be so subtle that you are unable to see them; only feeling them when your hands are gently resting upon their body. Hence if you were taught to give Reiki without touch, you may like to try finding out if placing your hands on your recipient, increases the level of feedback.

On the other hand bodily movements can become quite extreme. I have had a few clients who have felt compelled to open their arms outwards into a crucifix position and hold them there until the completion of the session. And one or two that have shaken their bodies to such an extreme, it doesn't look far off from convulsions.

Release of Tears

Whilst it is unusual for people to exhibit full-on crying, I would go so far as to say it is common for one or two quiet and gentle tears to fall. Naturally if you mostly close your eyes when giving Reiki, you may miss this happening, and sometimes you need to look quite closely because you may only be able to notice a tear beginning to form, though never be fully released.

It's another sign of processing and changes taking place. Excellent. It's working!

Frowning

You may notice someone frowning during a treatment, as they try to make sense of the energy changes they are perceiving, or as internal processing is taking place.

Relaxing the jaw

A slight parting of the lips will indicate that tension is being released in the client's jaw, and the energy of their body is changing.

Now whilst I hope the above can assist you in recognising changes taking place, naturally we also have to accept that you may experience the opposite. Where the client is completely still for a whole session and you think nothing much has happened.

Be assured I have experienced such instances and it could be that the recipient is not getting much from the treatment. However, it may just be that they'll later ask you whether they had their left leg extend ninety degrees off the table whilst you were wiping their forehead with a velvet pad, or want to know if the room had filled with a bright white light whilst you were at their knees, or tell you it felt as if their neck was being pulled straight when they knew full well you were standing at their feet with your hands on their ankles.

So do remember that a seeming lack of anything happening, is in no way confirmation of inactivity. It's simply that visible clues are at times comforting to acknowledge, and can help you to build your confidence.

Becoming Professional

Asking For Payment

Completion of Reiki Level Two training is the stage where you can choose to set up business as a Reiki Practitioner and work with the general public. If this is your way forward then one of the more testing conversations you must have with yourself is when and how much to charge for your services.

There is much discussion around the validity of being paid for Reiki and it has not been an area without struggle for me. Whilst my issues have been linked to the amount to be charged, for many the first stumbling block is being unwilling to charge for it at all. And the argument most often put forward in support of this position is that Reiki is a 'gift from God' or similar. The implication being that it is special (yes) and freely available (yes) and that it is spiritual (yes) and should therefore be given without charge (no).

Money is simply energy in a particular form, a method of exchange, and a convenient way of thanking somebody.

Naturally to a certain extent personal circumstances are going to dictate how you approach the aspect of payment. And ultimately I believe it all comes down to *balance* which is the epicentre of a well-led life.

A friend who has a very senior role in a blue chip company offers her healing skills as a volunteer at a hospice and it is obvious that this is a wonderful way in which she feels able to pay something back to the community. All credit to her. She doesn't require payment because her career pays her very well indeed and she is able to balance all that she receives in one environment, by giving back in another.

However, it is a little like the pensioner who goes to work at a charity shop without pay. Admirable as that is, it should not mean that everyone working in a retail environment should do so without their due remuneration. There is a difference between volunteering and having a career as a complementary therapist.

We Reiki Practitioners tend to be natural givers. But realise that when you give to excess, what began as a positive can soon become a negative as you go further from true equilibrium.

As a simple example, imagine that you like going out for coffee with a friend where your natural inclination may be to pay for the drinks. Nice. However, if you regularly go out for coffee with that same person, and *every* time you want to pay, your emotions are out of balance, partly through the act of over-giving and partly because you are actively denying your friend the pleasure of giving at all.

Be aware that finding it overly easy to give, whilst finding it extremely difficult to receive, might also be symptomatic of having an unhealthy need to control, because giving puts the giver in charge, whilst receiving is a form of allowing and therefore its opposite.

True self-awareness (central to Reiki) demands that we view our actions from the opposite side of what might, on the surface, be registered only as virtuous. Is there *overall* balance?

To be in balance, we really do need to allow ourselves to receive too. We have to value *ourselves* as much as others –

no one person more or less than anyone else, right? Are you valuing yourself and your time less than other people's, camouflaged by thoughts of doing good for others?

Always remember the flow of giving *and* receiving.

Of course there are going to be some instances where you wish to provide free or discounted treatments. I'm sure most of us would want to make exceptions for family, close friends, those in financial difficulties etc. I also reduce my rates for carers and colleagues at my place of work. Brilliant. But if you want to become a Reiki Practitioner then you have to accept you are in business. A heart-felt business, but a business nonetheless.

And if you require a little extra help in deciding to accept that you need to charge a fee, consider the following:

Failure to receive due payment will for most of us, strictly limit the number of people to whom we can offer Reiki, because it will remain a part-time hobby and never merit full-time dedication.

Not only will non-payment restrict the numbers of people that you'll be able to offer Reiki to, but I also believe that it will restrict the amount of help you will likely be able to give them. If you think about it, when you are offering Reiki for free, the recipient will almost certainly be feeling very grateful to you for their first appointment, and that may well be true if they accept a second. But actually, if it were you, how would you feel about asking someone for a third, fourth or fifth appointment if it were such a totally one-sided arrangement? Would there be a point, where you would say to yourself, *"I just don't think I could ask them **again**?"* This inevitably means that in cases where a person would benefit by an extended course of treatments, they would most likely deny themselves the opportunity.

Receiving payment for Reiki and putting your service on a business footing gives permission for greater honesty, which is a vital part of the relationship between recipient and Practitioner.

When no value is applied, the receiver will likely feel under a lot of pressure to say how great things are and how well they are doing out of feeling indebted to the giver. *"They've gone to all that trouble on my behalf, I can't possibly let them down by telling them that I don't feel any better."*

"How have things been since your last appointment?"

"Oh very good. Thank you so much."

When we have paid for a service however, we tend to be more comfortable with expressing our true position.

"How have things been since your last appointment?"

"Well I have had a really bad week this week. In fact my back feels worse than it did three weeks ago."

It may not be what you would like to hear, but at least you know.

Actually, if you are ever met with a similar response, do delve deeper. Context is always important and so you need to establish if the lack of progress is against a backdrop of the status quo, or a change in circumstances...

"Is there any additional activity that you have been doing since I last saw you?"

"No...

...Oh yes. I had to do all that weeding in the garden because if you remember it was a lovely day last Tuesday. And then of course Mark and Ellie were moving house and so I was helping them with the big items..."

Or maybe it just stops at the *"no"*; better to know.

There is a tendency to just be grateful when no payment is made. I value honesty more.

Essentially we aren't really charging for Reiki – that's priceless. But there is a calculable value for the cost of hiring a treatment venue or the heating and lighting costs if you work from home. Also for petrol, laundry, insurance premiums, membership of any organisations (such as the UK Reiki Federation, The Reiki Association etc.) and advertising your services – such as printing leaflets or running a website. Finally, remember the need to cover the investment you made in your training and are now making in your time.

And if you struggle with that last item on the list, and fail to value your time, it may be that you are failing to value yourself. Just saying!

Consider too how when we pay for something, we value it more highly. This can be key where you are galvanising the resources of a person to invest in their own health and well-being. It is a human trait to want value for money. We treat free and/or cheap things differently from those with a higher price tag. When we think something has cost us, we want to see results and we put more of our resources into proving to ourselves that our outlay was a sound one.

Scientific research has proved this difference in perception. Be aware that surprisingly for many people, there will be a tangible benefit in paying say £1.35 for a brand named paracetamol as opposed to thirty pence for the equivalent supermarket version (even where the product is like for like), purely on the basis that for most of us, the branded product is reasoned to be superior and therefore its results will be too. Even though this rationale is often taking place on a *completely unconscious* level and we can logically agree that there should be no difference except to our pocket, tests have revealed otherwise.

People will often heal more easily when they feel they have invested in the 'best' available to them.

This leads me on nicely to the monetary issue that has featured far more in my own relationship with Reiki, which is how *much* to charge for my services.

Now I have struggled with not feeling 'good enough' most of my life and guess that a large number of you would also be raising your hand to that one.

Having thought that I had made fantastic strides in my life by reducing the effects of this pernicious trait, along came Reiki and revealed that it had simply been having a bit of break and, after a short siesta, was ready to party long and hard into the night. So I have spent many years undervaluing my services, by charging low prices and feeling pretty awful every time it got to the point of asking for payment.

It actually causes me embarrassment when I think back to just how low my rates were over an extended period of time. Years of feeling that what *I* offered couldn't be deemed to be of high enough quality to receive reasonable payment for it. I had no doubt that Reiki was worth a great deal, it was purely my delivery of it that was in question.

I loved it when a client would begin taking out their purse or wallet at the end of an appointment, before I had to raise the tricky issue myself. When that didn't happen (was that because they were in a lovely floaty state from the Reiki or was it for my spiritual learning that I was *made to ask* for payment?) I felt like my back was against the wall. *"Oh no, I'm going to have to remind them that they owe me for the treatment."* It would be so stressful for me that I would contemplate whether it was easier simply to not say anything and just see it as a bonus if they remembered later and paid after the event.

What I was really doing was under-valuing *myself*. Interestingly this was not typical of my working life in general. Perhaps it would have been understandable had I always been low-paid. However, for most of my previous career I had worked in the City of London and been amply rewarded for doing so.

Fascinating how the underlying beliefs that we unconsciously carry are complex things; they can be very specific in their application. A handsome salary was readily forthcoming when working as a Product Manager. I probably felt I deserved it for doing a job I felt was hard work, which required an alarm clock familiar with the early hour settings and also included quite a lot of stress. So my issue had to be specifically around some aspect of being a Reiki therapist. How much do I deserve whilst doing something that gives me great pleasure? How much do I deserve when I can't guarantee what the results will be? How much do I deserve when it is impossible to benchmark my abilities against anyone else's?

When I finally began believing I was good enough to raise my prices, do you know what happened? I got more clients. Yes, more, not fewer.

But, as with anything in life, you have to feel it for yourself. No one can tell you.

Actually people can tell you because friends and fellow Practitioners did exactly that, clearly stating that my fees should be raised. And yet as they expressed this, it was as if they were talking about someone else. It bore no relation to me. I could hear the words but not feel them. My agreement to them was always in principle and therefore for others, not for myself.

Occasionally even *clients* told me that they thought I was asking for too little. I would smile and think how very kind they were, but could not accept the truth in their words.

If you recognise this in yourself, realise that it is touching on some deeply held (and erroneous) belief that you are not good enough. Understand that when you hear the same thing expressed by more than one source, it is a way of giving yourself a message. It's time to take notice. That in itself is unfortunately unlikely to simply switch on the button that permits you to make the appropriate change. But please use it to begin to take action *in the direction of that change* and apply yourself mentally and emotionally towards doing so.

I sense that I received an increase in appointments when I valued myself sufficiently that my clients could too. Equally if I had originally over-valued myself and reflected that over-valuation by inflating appointment charges, my diary might have looked distinctly empty for that very reason. The Universe has a way of making us face that which we need to face for our ultimate benefit.

It was therefore probably appropriate for me to start out with a low figure. No kidding myself that I was an expert from day one because the real training in Reiki comes from the experience of working with people.

Reiki asks you to have an honest relationship with yourself and a large part of that relationship for many of us will be awareness and then development of our own self-worth.

To establish an appropriate value for your services, I suggest investigating the charges quoted in your local area both for Reiki and therapies that are broadly similar, such as Massage and Reflexology. At the time of writing, an average for an hour long treatment in the area in which I live is £40 - £45. (From this guideline price you can then consider if it feels appropriate to charge the same or a little differently, depending on your circumstances.)

Certification & Legislation

Deciding on your fee is the beginning of putting your services on a business footing. The title of Reiki Practitioner will need you to additionally consider the following:

Certification & Insurance

At the end of each level of your training, you should receive a certificate from your Reiki Teacher. Receiving your Reiki Level Two certification (well done!) will enable you to work with members of the public, although being insured is naturally also a prerequisite to doing so. Please be aware that you may struggle finding insurance if you have learnt Reiki via an online course because some insurers may require you to have had a face-to-face attunement.

An insurance company will require copies of your certificates before underwriting a policy.

You will require both professional indemnity insurance, and public liability insurance. These can be arranged either directly with an appropriate insurance company, or sometimes via membership of a professional body. If the former, it is helpful to approach a company that specialises in cover for complementary therapists (I use Balens Ltd.). If the latter, than becoming a member of an organisation such as The Reiki Association or UK

Reiki Federation, may offer you access to a block (and therefore discounted) insurance scheme.

Professional indemnity insurance is designed to cover your business for compensation claims made by a client where you've made a mistake in your work or there's been a level of professional negligence on your part. This would include instances such as breaches of confidentiality, or the losing of client documents or data.

Public liability insurance is designed to cover your business for compensation claims made by a client due to injury or property damage. This would include instances of a client hurting themselves, such as by falling as they get off the therapy table, or tripping over an electric cable in your therapy room.

Be aware too, that if you are choosing to work from home, your household insurance policy is likely to require amendment to accommodate this. Additionally you will need to check that you will not be in breach of any home loan (mortgage) or rental agreement, and that you are adhering to any local authority by-laws.

If by working from home you are choosing to work in a wooden cabin in your garden, please raise this with any potential insurer, because wooden structures may require a particular level of cover when allocated to business use, due to the perceived increase in fire risk.

Should you choose to work from any kind of therapy centre, it is likely they will ask you to provide duplicates of both your qualifications and your insurance policy.

Although I have never been asked, a potential client would also be perfectly within their rights to request to view your credentials before they book an appointment with you. Be aware though that insurance companies may ask you *not to highlight* that you have cover, in order to avoid unscrupulous claims against you.

Taxation

As soon as you begin to receive money in exchange for your services, you are responsible for filing the appropriate financial details, to ensure you pay the relevant government tax. If you are working in the UK then contact HMRC (Her Majesty's Revenue and Customs) to register and also for helpful on advice on your legal obligations.

Don't panic if you have never had to do anything like this before. Once registered (usually as being self-employed), it broadly comes down to listing the income you receive, together with your business expenditure to show all of your costs.

Do set up a bank account specifically for your work, although there is no requirement for it to be acknowledged as a business bank account where you would be charged commission on every transaction. Just an ordinary standard current account is all you need – enabling you to show the incomings and outgoings via a bank statement.

Keep every bank statement and receipt for any items purchased directly for your business, as proof for your records. Currently UK law specifies that you must retain all pertinent financial information for a minimum of seven years. Ensure you make duplicates of any documentation you file with your tax office, so that you can refer to it in the case of any queries or disputes.

If the joys of finances elude you, then my best advice is to keep your financial information up-to-date. The stress free way is to do it little and often. It will likely take less than an hour each month. But if you don't do it for a while, not only does it become a major project, it can also be hard to remember what on earth that faded £6.99 receipt was for. It might annoy you for a full day and a half before you remember it was your business diary.

Note that if you choose to work from home, as well as being responsible for registering and paying your income tax, you may also be liable to pay business rates, so do check any local government regulations.

Lineage

Your learning lineage is the line of teaching descendants from the founder Mikao Usui, to your own teacher, so I guess you could call it your Reiki family tree.

Whilst most professional organisations demand sight of your certificates coupled with your insurance documentation (if you will not be arranging it via them), prior to offering membership, they (and even some Reiki Facebook groups) may additionally request you provide them with your lineage, and it will be considered a necessity should you choose to register with a regulatory body.

If your teacher did not provide this at the time of your training, it is worth approaching them now to gain a copy, whilst you hopefully still have their contact details. If you are reading this after having just trained on your First Degree of Reiki, consider checking in advance that the teacher for your Second Degree will provide this. And if you trained a while ago to Reiki Second Degree or Reiki Master Level, and are at a loss as to how to contact your teacher to request your lineage retrospectively, then you can approach The Reiki Association, Reiki Council or UK Reiki Federation who may be able to help you via a tracing service. (At the time of writing, the UK Reiki Federation charge a £20 fee for their assistance, and will refund £10 of the fee if they are unsuccessful.)

Professional Organisations

Certainly not a necessity – there is currently no obligation to join a professional body – however membership of such an organisation may provide a level of reassurance to potential clients.

Additionally there are some work venues which might stipulate membership as a pre-condition, because you are then likely to meet with an acceptable level of professionalism and abide by a suitable code of ethics.

If you are even remotely considering the possibility of joining a professional body, and you are still training, it is therefore well worth ensuring that your course is appropriately accredited, and will provide you with their basic entry requirements.

Membership can be helpful from your perspective too as they are often a very good way in which to keep up-to-date with any legal requirements. I list below the UK treatment restrictions at the time of writing, as an example of how the UK Reiki Federation can provide important guidelines to abide by:

- ❖ "The following diseases are notifiable under the Health Protection (Notification) Regulations 2010:
    Acute encephalitis, acute meningitis, acute poliomyelitis, acute infectious hepatitis, anthrax, botulism, brucellosis, cholera, diphtheria, enteric fever (typhoid or paratyphoid fever), food poisoning, haemolytic uraemic syndrome (HUS), infectious bloody diarrhoea, invasive group A streptococcal disease and scarlet fever, legionnaires' disease, leprosy, malaria, measles, meningococcal septicaemia, mumps, plague, rabies, rubella, SARS, smallpox, tetanus, tuberculosis, typhus, viral haemorrhagic fever (VHF), whooping cough, yellow fever."

- ❖ "It is an offence to advertise in any way (either in writing or verbally) that might lead to someone seeking treatment for:

Bright's Disease, Cataract, Cancer, Diabetes, Epilepsy or fits, Glaucoma, Locomotor Ataxy, Paralysis, or Tuberculosis.

The 1939 Cancer Act also specifically makes it an offence to prescribe any treatments for the disease, or to give advice in connection to cancer treatment.

However naturally it is perfectly acceptable to provide Reiki sessions for anyone who is experiencing these conditions."

(In the case of the UK's Cancer Act, the key intention is to protect the vulnerable from being sold 'cures'. It is as much aimed at pharmaceutical companies, as at complementary therapists and is designed to prevent anyone from claiming that they can 'treat' cancer. There is no similar law in the U.S.A for example, so it is always worth investigating your own country's legislation.)

- ❖ "Reiki Practitioners must not attend women in childbirth or give them Reiki for ten days thereafter unless they hold an appropriate qualification in midwifery. Or unless the client, in consultation with a practising midwife or a Registered Medical Practitioner, requests their services."

- "Reiki can only be given to patients in hospitals with permission of the patient, or the person authorised to make decisions on their behalf, together with the person responsible for their medical care. Reiki Practitioners must not give the impression that they are a medical professional or a member of hospital staff."

As well as imparting useful knowledge, a professional organisation can also help you to feel like part of a community of therapists. This can be very encouraging, especially when being a Practitioner can feel quite isolating.

The UK Reiki Federation, for instance, issues a regular magazine which includes contributed articles from other Practitioners. It keeps its readers informed of differing Reiki applications, such as working in hospitals or with animals, and so on. It also provides access to "Reiki Share" groups, where you can meet up with fellow Practitioners, swap treatments, share experiences etc. Many "Shares" do exist outside of the main associations though, so it's worth doing a general Internet search for groups in your area, if this appeals.

Music (Public Performance) Licenses

Something that needs consideration is the legality of your playing music in a therapy situation. In the UK there are two types of licenses to be aware of:

PRS for Music (the Performing Rights Society) which represents songwriters, composers and music publishers.

PPL (Phonographic Performance Limited) which licenses the use of recorded music being played in public.

Each organisation has a website allowing you to clarify to what extent their licensing will apply, ensuring you comply with the Copyright, Designs and Patents Act 1988.

It may be that renting a therapy room means that you are covered by the license of the owner, however, don't take this for granted.

If your business means you carry out home visits, then taking music to play would require a license, although the client could play their own music without any infringement of copyright.

One way to overcome the issue is to purchase royalty free music. This will however come at a premium because effectively you are paying for a license to play the music within the purchase price. It also greatly restricts the choice available.

One further key aspect of legislation that you are required to abide by, is data protection for any client details you hold – so read on.

The Consultation

Prior to your first appointment, you are going to have to put together a Client Record or Consultation Form. This must meet with your insurance company's requirements. You may therefore need to refer to your policy, to ensure you collate the minimum information they require.

The completion of a Client Record will also result in a need to abide by any data protection legislation of the country in which you operate. However, be aware the General Data Protection Regulation (GDPR) 2018, covers not only businesses operating in EU (European Union) countries, but also EU citizens. It therefore becomes necessary to conform to GDPR if you are treating any EU citizen, even if your business is based outside of the EU itself.

One aspect of GDPR is concerned with ensuring that no company holds data about anyone, where it is no longer in the direct interests of the individual concerned. This results in Client Records being securely destroyed seven years after the last occasion on which a treatment was given. (This timeframe corresponds to the time limit applying to legal action for breach of contract.)

However my insurance company would prefer the retention of any records that relate to the treatment of children, for a period of seven years *after* they have reached the age of majority. (In the UK, this is eighteen years of age.) And for those with learning difficulties, where there is no statute of limitations, it requests I consider keeping them ad infinitum.

Whilst the current lack of clarity is frustrating when wishing to provide you with the best level of detail for your business, it does at least raise the point that legislation is not static. It will change over the course of the life of your business. It is therefore a timely reminder to keep up-to-date with *current* legislation. Because we are talking about the law, *you* must be entirely confident that you are meeting all of *your* responsibilities.

In the UK, the Information Commissioner's Office (ICO) is the organisation to refer any queries you have regarding your data protection obligations. In some circumstances, you may need to register with the ICO – if you visit their website you can complete a short questionnaire that will confirm your particular status. (At the time of writing if you are a sole trader then you are likely to remain exempt. If, for any reason this proves not to be the case, then the ICO current charge is £40 per year.)

There is no part of the data protection laws that specifically regulate our, or any other, industry sector. Accordingly the regulations are more general in nature, and place the onus upon the individual in charge of the data to determine what can be considered a reasonable level of protection, in each and every circumstance.

For instance, if you are holding client data electronically, an appropriate level of security might be password protection on your computer. Whilst if transferring data from your computer to a third party, particularly where sensitive health records are concerned, it's likely to be considered reasonable to ensure that the data is encrypted.

Choosing to maintain manual (handwritten) records means I can avoid electronic security concerns. And because manual documentation is my preferred route, I'll cover the major considerations when adopting this style of record keeping.

(Just so you know, I store my client records in a locked filing cabinet which is kindly provided at my place of work. Before that was an option, however, I used to use a lockable metal document box which you can buy for between £10 and £20.)

When compiling your documentation you might like to replicate the structure I use, which consists of four main sections:

Section One - Data gathering, consent and basic client details.

GDPR stipulates that we must first gain consent to collect information about our clients. Whilst this is a requirement for businesses in general, it is naturally particularly important in ours because details about an individual's health are considered as 'special category' personal data.

A client's consent for us to gather this information needs to be explicitly given, and therefore must be sought at the beginning of any appointment. Clients need to understand why we are requesting the information, what it will be used for, who will have sight of it and how long it will be held for. The highly sensitive nature of the data, requires that the client is also ensured of complete confidentiality, which needs to be clearly stated.

Accordingly, even before taking the name and address of a client, I now request permission to do so, in the following format:

"The General Data Protection Regulation of 2018, asks me to make clear the following:

*All personal data is collected **only** for the specific purpose of carrying out this, and any future Reiki treatments, so as to provide the highest level of service. Any medical history you share is recorded only with a view to ensuring the most effective treatment is provided.*

*All data is **completely confidential** and will never be shared with any third party. It will be held for the minimum lawful and contractual period. When disposed of, this will be handled securely (shredded).*

You have the right to view the data, and request amendments.

I give my consent:

Name_____ Signature _____

Date ___/___/_____"

Another important factor regarding GDPR is that any marketing activity must be specifically authorised by a client. Whereas in the past, I simply treated it as a courtesy to contact a client the day after their first treatment (and in instances where there appears to be a strong reaction to a treatment), to find out how they were feeling, this now has to have been explicitly agreed to in advance. Because many clients text me to request appointments, my form now includes the following statements, with a tick box beside each one:

"I am happy to receive a text or call:

- ❖ *Following a treatment to check how I am responding.*
- ❖ *To confirm/amend the scheduling of appointments."*

Similarly, if you would like to contact your client base advertising say a new offer, approval must have been expressly given beforehand. You will be required to request permission for each individual reason you wish to get in touch with a client, so they understand exactly what they are agreeing to. It is not acceptable to have a general statement that would cover a range of different reasons for communication. Please note that this new legislation has an impact on past clients because they too must now specifically authorise you to contact them, and on what basis. You would therefore need to contact them initially to ask for permission and gain their written consent to later sending them a marketing communication – every purpose of which must be explicitly detailed.

Clients now have a specific right to view the information you hold on them, and request amendments to what is written. Any such request must be dealt with within one month from the date it is made. Should a client ever request a copy of their Client Record, this needs to provided free of charge, and given to the client in a sealed envelope with the client's name clearly displayed, together with the words 'Private and Confidential'.

Having gained permission to request personal information, I then gather the more traditional details:

- ❖ Client Name.
- ❖ Address including postal (zip) code.
- ❖ Telephone Number(s) (mobile/landline).
- ❖ Date of Birth.
- ❖ Occupation.
- ❖ Client's doctor (name and surgery) in case of emergency. (Actually this specific piece of information is gathered by the Receptionist at the centre in which I work, but if you are working solo you may want to include it.)

Section Two – All the contractual things, (including disclaimers, recommendations and signatures.)

Gathering the signature of a client at this stage of the document ensures you have written permission to carry out a treatment. This signature can also be used to confirm they have had sight of any disclaimers that you want to make in advance. These should include the fact that a Reiki treatment is not designed to diagnose a condition. Nor can it be used to prescribe or adjust medication. This remains the remit of their General Practitioner (doctor), who must be consulted for any acute or infectious condition, or any health issue that causes the client concern. I make it very clear that there can never be any guarantee as to the outcome of any treatment, or course of treatments.

A further disclaimer stipulates that any advice I give during treatment is done with the best intention, but that it remains the responsibility of the client to choose to accept it, or act upon it in anyway.

I use this section to highlight how Reiki may generate feelings of light-headedness and request the client ensures they are fully alert before getting down from the therapy couch, or before they drive anywhere. I advise the client to drink plenty of water on the day of a treatment (as long as this follows any hydration advice given by their GP).

You may wonder whether, in instances where you have already gained the dated signature of the client for data protection purposes, you need to have it again on this section of the form. The short answer is yes. GDPR makes it very clear that any consent regarding a person's data must remain completely separate from their consent for anything else, such as for treatment. The client is required to sign twice, one signature to cover each aspect in turn.

(It's worth noting that initially I split the front page of my Client Record so that the information from section one and section two were both on the same piece of paper. Then I noticed how many clients would read (or at least scan) the top half of the form (GDPR) and sign, but would feel overwhelm by the time they got to the second half. This meant they were failing to read about many important aspects of accepting a treatment. There's no magic formula, however progress has been made by having a separate sheet for the GDPR. Once read, signed and returned to me, I then take down their personal details on my Client Record document. This provides a natural break before asking them to read and sign again for section two, resulting in a greater chance of them absorbing the details.)

There are times when it won't be the client who is signing – it will be the parent or guardian. In such instances I supplement my form with a further document. This confirms that a parent or guardian may be committing a criminal offence if they fail to provide adequate medical aid for their child, and that they must consult a doctor concerning the health of that child, because Reiki is not defined as medical aid in UK law. (See chapter Working With Young People.)

A few eyebrows have been raised by the parent on my requesting their signature, due to the severity of the wording. Those same eyebrows are quickly lowered, when I point out it is to protect a child from receiving Reiki rather than say a plaster cast, should they have broken their leg etc.

Section Three – Information gathering and delivering.

It's natural to begin by asking someone why they have come for an appointment. I allow plenty of space on my form for me to write down their response, because it may cover a range of physical and emotional issues, as well as their medical and personal history.

I like to gather details of the client's feelings and emotions around their situation, as much as the facts of their circumstances. It can be very revealing to see and hear how someone does or doesn't express themselves. The lovely thing is that of course if someone is uncomfortable expressing much about their situation, or is unable to do so – be that through trauma, or their lack of resources (a baby or young child for instance) – then with Reiki that's no problem.

Nowadays I'm confident of eliciting the information without prompts, but early on it was beneficial to have a few stock questions to ask and to list them on my form. These would remind me, when a client listed a physical reason for seeking Reiki, to ask about their emotional well-being and vice versa. It prompted me to ask if they are seeing a doctor (or suggest they should) about their condition – ensuring I confirmed I have no medical training and am not qualified to offer any form of diagnosis. It reminded me to ask them if they knew the trigger for their imbalance (can they avoid it in the future?) and so on.

When you're a few minutes into the consultation, it can be useful to ask them if they sense that they can make any changes in their life, to help themselves in anyway. Asking them to 'sense' a response, enhances the likelihood of their reaching their own inner wisdom, because they will be less likely to look to their logical mind for the answer – although it may be very logical advice they give themselves.

For instance "*I know I should go to bed earlier*" or "*I know I should socialise more rather than play video games all the time*". Get them to hear that message, value it and then act on it. I'll highlight that this is their own inner wisdom speaking, and empower them with the knowledge that they will usually know the best way to help themselves. Reiki treatments are often about raising levels of self-awareness and self-care and most importantly, self-love.

There are times when a client extends the consultation stage beyond the norm. Then it's useful to intuitively sense the energy around the exchange, because realising why that might be happening, may help you to help them more…

Where this dialogue is offering an uncommon opportunity for a client to open up, it's literally possible to feel the energy release taking place as they allow that to happen. Equally the healing may also be coming from the fact they are being listened to (note-taking sometimes has to be put on hold whilst full eye contact is observed). I give them as much time as they need to express themselves as fully as they wish. When hearing particularly challenging stories, it's good to remember we're not there to give advice. So there's no pressure to come up with some sort of answer or resolution; there is power just in acknowledging all that they have gone through. At times I've found it beneficial to remind them that they have survived the incident(s), and how strong and resourceful they must be to have done so. However, when faced with extremely distressing accounts – such as when one young woman told me that she had been raped twice whilst travelling abroad – I have often found I am only able thank the person for feeling they could share their story with me. Actually that has always felt to be enough. Sometimes we are just there to do no more than act as a witness.

Extended consultations may be the sign that a client is experiencing a level of anxiety which is making it hard for them to stop talking. Here my aim is to help them to feel safe in silence; to relax into 'being' rather than 'doing'. They may benefit from your intervention – asking them to slow down as they talk and to breathe more deeply as they do so.

Then again, they may be revealing themselves to be a person who's allowing their past to have too big a role in defining their future. They have become too wrapped up in the emotional turmoil that certain events have created in their life. They have to repeat their story regularly, to justify maintaining the level of anger, hurt or sadness they still carry inside them. I might feel led, where this feels the case, to gently point their awareness to the present and future.

Moving them more quickly to the therapy bed, helps to begin to break the pattern.

It's worth repeating, that whilst these observations may help assess how long to provide before you move a client to the therapy couch, you do not need to resolve the issues themselves. The Reiki energy is going to be doing that.

Naturally the exact opposite can be true. A client may not want to talk. This might be because it is just too emotionally painful to do so. Alternatively it may happen when an individual has been through a lot of hospital appointments and/or other therapy sessions – they are tired by having to re-explain themselves, and are wanting just to establish how much Reiki might work for them. In such cases, of course, we have the lovely advantage of being able to work without the details.

Ultimately everyone is unique – there can be no specific formula for how any session should pan out. Such individuality also means you can never know exactly how someone else feels, so I avoid ever pretending that I can.

I remember once, hearing on the radio about a railway employee. He was being celebrated for saving someone from taking their own life. He was remarkably modest, and explained that his ability to have done so mostly came from a workplace training programme he had attended. It had included how to talk to someone in that specific situation. The instructor had made it very clear that the worst thing you could say was "*I know how you feel"* because that could be vehemently denied, and rapport instantly lost.

We all feel differently.

In a similar vein, I believe it is important not to undermine the legitimacy of a person's feelings, by stating they should handle their situation differently. This would imply they are doing things wrong, or badly, and how do we know?

This raises how important it is to be ever vigilant about any verbal communication you have with your clients. *Feel* the energy of your words. You can then tell if you have explained something in a way that empowers the person in front of you, or has made them feel vulnerable. Be ever mindful never to promote fear.

As a Practitioner we have to consider the subtlety of expression, which can radically change tone. Note the difference between saying *"if something similar was happening to me, I might…"* rather than *"if I were you I would…"* The former takes ownership of my thoughts, feelings and actions without in anyway demeaning theirs. It opens a new possibility rather than closing down an existing one. I'm not then dis-empowering them by making it sound as if they should be doing something they are not. I'm not suggesting, or even worse, telling someone else what to do.

After all, telling someone *"you should"* do something is the most likely way to trigger their rebellious streak, even if what follows really would be a good idea. Whereas there can be no rebellion against someone saying what *they* would do. Such a statement comes from a neutral standpoint to be accepted or rejected. It also avoids bad advice, meant well, because it is impossible for us to ever truly place ourselves in another person's shoes. We can imagine what it would be like and empathise with their circumstances, but we cannot know fully what it is like to be them.

Actions that would make sense in our world, with our family and our friends, may be impossible, impractical or downright inadvisable in their circumstances.

Furthermore it is important that people take responsibility for the choices they make in their life. If you suggest a response and it does not work out favourably, then you are helping someone to lay blame at your door. *"You said I should _____ and now look where I am!"* Our Reiki training does not equip us to be a counsellor and occasionally we need to remind ourselves of that.

It is why it is good to feel connected to Reiki before you even greet the person who has come to you for treatment. This way you are working in a state of love and compassion. Those emotional states will help you over-ride any instances where perhaps you express a common turn of phrase, only to realise that it is actually quite negative and restrictive, rather than the positive and uplifting, perfectly constructed sentence you would have chosen to compose.

Of course, even after more than a decade in the business, I can still mess up and phrase things badly. It's then served me well to take a deep breath and sense connecting more fully into the guidance of my Soul energy, asking for increased direction, and for words to come *through* me, rather than *from* me, surrendering more completely to a wisdom much greater than my own.

Comfortingly, research confirms that people respond far more to *how* you say something, than to *what* you say. Therefore as we are working from the heart, we mustn't berate ourselves over slip-ups (where we realise we've said something in less than perfect terms), because thankfully the *intention* behind the words will not have been lost. Hence why it is important to *feel the energy* of what we are saying.

Working in the *energy of the moment*, rather than attempting to pre-plan any form of strategy, will improve the chances of you helping your clients more effectively. I raise this because I've noticed that the more I tried to pre-structure the consultation part of the session, the less well it went. This makes sense because of course I would be failing to work *in the client's current energy* on the day, and trying instead to work in *what I think it will be*.

For instance a strategy suggested to one client and met with such enthusiasm that I would look to engineer it into a conversation with another client experiencing similar issues, would then be met with not even a modicum of interest. What is helpful to one client at one moment during a conversation, cannot necessarily be replicated later with another.

In a similar vein when I have cut out an article that I thought would really appeal to a client, such as on the benefits of Reiki for those with Multiple Sclerosis, and be *determined* to give it to them, it was as if it was their cue to look highly uninterested in it. Perhaps I'd hand it over to them, they'd thank me, but instead of reading even just its title, they would stuff it in their handbag, and talk with great animation about something else completely. Now that doesn't mean I won't take an article for someone. But now I focus my energy on delivering it, *only if it feels right* to do so. This may mean that it is two sessions down the road when I hand it over – or it may be placed in my recycling bin without ever being passed on.

It can be true even of strategies such as recommending meditation classes. I might think *"oh, I must remember to mention the possible value of meditation to x when I next see them."* Then, if at their next appointment, I sense that it shouldn't be spoken about, instead of attempting to force it and bring it unnaturally into the conversation I just let it go. Sometimes I don't even have to consciously let it go, because I just forget to say anything. Then, rather than being cross at myself for not remembering, I affirm how it obviously wasn't right to talk about it – trusting that it would have come to mind if it were meant to do so.

You may therefore notice that some people will change so radically between appointments that you will have been wanting to raise a point with the person as they were when you last saw them, when what you should be doing is talking to the one who has just walked in the door that day. Recognise that you should be talking to them now from their new perspective and way of being/feeling. Brilliant. There's been progress, and we need to honour their new self and support that change.

Being a Reiki Practitioner means going with the flow.

As a general rule, on the first consultation, when it feels as if everything the client wants to mention has been mentioned, I will then ask *"is there anything else you would like to share?"* It can be a very valuable add-on question, which helps people to open up a little more, providing a further opportunity for their own self-awareness, as much as my understanding.

Depending on the circumstances, (though mostly in cases where there would be an obvious advantage to change them to a more positive *emotional* state), I may then ask a client to confirm what they are seeking to gain from the treatment. They will have just listed all the things that they almost definitely don't want in their life – those ways in which it has not been working well – *"I'm sad, lonely, and angry"*. Then it can be wonderful to help them to set an intention for what they *do* want.

However it has to be achievable – a *small* step towards an improved *inner emotional state* and not a step (small or otherwise) to a change of circumstance. Because if the person concerned is say a Carer for someone else, a change of circumstances may be completely unrealistic. And generally, whilst setting an intention can be helpful, we never know what the result of a Reiki treatment will be. It can therefore be counter-productive to set specific expectations. I'm talking here therefore about an aim to *"feel calmer"*, *"feel more peaceful"*, *"more energised"* or similar.

Labelling the wanted emotion, as well as focusing the energy for the session, is also more likely to enable a client's inner wisdom to come up with relevant solutions. It may additionally enable me to make a helpful suggestion. For instance, if ultimately the client seeks *"more joy"* in their life, I might ask them what pursuits they've found joyous in the past. That in turn may remind them of a once-held passion for drawing or dancing, which I could then encourage them to revisit.

Having gathered the major details, I usually also establish a client's sleeping pattern. Good regular sleep is so often a foundation for balance in mind and body. Reminding a client of its importance can therefore be of value.

There are a couple of practical questions that are worth asking. One is how they have heard about you (recommendation, leaflet, website etc.) which enables you to assess which advertising strategy is working best for you. Another is whether they have received Reiki before, which will assist you in establishing how much you'll be required to explain the structure of the treatment itself.

Should it be their first Reiki treatment, then it's good to agree or inform them of the following:

- ❖ That they will be asked to remove their shoes, and glasses if they wear them.
- ❖ The bodily position in which they will receive the Reiki. (Whether they are best remaining seated, or lying on their back, front or side on the therapy couch.)
- ❖ Would they prefer music to be played or not? (If you offer this option.)

- ❖ Whether touch will form part of the treatment (and if so assurance that there will be no touch involved on any intimate part of the body).
- ❖ Confirmation they can move during the treatment, and that their body may make unconscious movements as a way of re-aligning or releasing trauma.
- ❖ How they can discuss any aspect with you during the treatment if necessary. Their comfort and ease is your main consideration.
- ❖ That it's fine to open their eyes at any point if they would like to do so.
- ❖ How, if they are comfortable closing their eyes, this will help them to relax more deeply. And this in turn may allow them to see the beautiful colours Reiki often brings, together with any images provided by their unconscious/Soul/Inner Being.
- ❖ That a Reiki Practitioner is not required to work necessarily at the specific place of imbalance/trauma.
- ❖ Whilst it is impossible to describe in advance what they will experience, because it is so individual (and they may feel nothing at all), a range of common sensations are:

    Warmth and/or coolness

    Tingling

    Physical pressure

    Twitching

    Stomach gurgling (to be welcomed as a sign of their body responding!)

Weightlessness/heaviness

And over-riding all of these, are usually feelings of deep relaxation, peacefulness and calm.

Having discussed the above it's then a good idea to ask if anything you have mentioned has raised any questions. Should they raise one, remember that a perfectly acceptable answer can be that you don't know, or that you believe something to be the case, though it is only your current understanding, or what you have been led to believe from your training. Not every question about Reiki can be given a categorical answer.

When the client is in the appropriate position it is then good to ascertain:

- ❖ Would they like a blanket?
- ❖ Do they require any adjustment to pillow height at their head or under their knees? (Lifting a person's knees slightly by use of a pillow, will support their back on the therapy couch.)

Section 4 – Treatment programme.

It's vital to keep a record of the date of every treatment. Write up a summary of what occurred during each session including results, feedback, experiences and any advice given. Make sure any advice falls within your remit as a Reiki Practitioner, or any other therapy that you are both trained and insured for.

Remember that a client is within their rights to request sight of their notes. Also that they might be used in the (highly unlikely) event of any legal action being sought against you. Do therefore ensure any comments are professional in both tone and content.

As well as securely destroying (which is likely to mean shredding) Client Records when they cease to be required for legal reasons, remember to make appropriate arrangements for their disposal in the event of your death.

And I'm sure it is an unnecessary point to make, but every detail shared between you and a client is, and must remain, *entirely confidential*. So never divulge any aspect of a client's relationship with you to anyone else. Ensuring that includes any members of a client's family.

The only scenario where an exception might apply is if a client threatened suicide. In such cases there is a legal obligation to raise the issue with the relevant health professional (GP or psychiatrist). The client concerned must be made aware of the action taken, and the treatment record you hold for them, updated appropriately.

Making An Appointment

With the framework for your business and your appointments in place, you can look forward to beginning to truly work as a Reiki Practitioner. Since many people, however, receive their first client before properly advertising themselves – through a referral from a friend or family member – we'll look at marketing yourself shortly, and dive in to what's involved in making an appointment.

When you first get a call, text or email from a prospective client (yippee, congratulations!) remember you are already working with them at an energetic level. It doesn't happen when they've booked an appointment and are standing in front of you. The energy exchange will have begun from when they first came across your name – there will be some energetic vibration that will have led them to contact you in the first place. Build on this, and ensure that you provide a level of service and care from the very start.

This means being well organised and getting back to people promptly whenever they are trying to get hold of you. It's therefore important (if you advertise your email address), to check your spam folder a little more thoroughly and regularly than you may have done in the past. Additionally, if you have any 'missed calls' showing up on your mobile phone, ring them back and find out if they are a potential client who didn't feel comfortable leaving a voicemail.

I have found it very useful to highlight both on my website and leaflets, that I am happy for people to send me a text message. This gives those who are unsettled by phone calls and voicemails an easy way of getting in contact. (Many of my clients come to me with issues of anxiety. Enough said.)

When starting out, it can be beneficial to have a list of the key things to mention or ask when you receive any interest in your services. I kept a piece of paper in my diary with the salient points, so that nerves or the shock of someone phoning when I least expected it, wouldn't make my mind go blank making me seem less than professional. If they're emailing you've got time to think about these things, if they are phoning you then you haven't.

The main things noted on that paper were:

Their Phone Number

I realise that it should come up in the phone log on a modern smart phone, but I have had instances where for some reason my phone hasn't saved the number, and actually when I started out mobiles weren't that clever.

Treat them as gold dust. If you can't get back to someone due to a phone malfunction or a lost written note, then it would be all too easy for your reputation to become tarnished. *"Oh they never got back to me, try somebody else."*

Time and Date of the Appointment

I know it is unlikely that you will forget to arrange these particular details, but a list is a list, and it may as well be complete.

The Venue

If you are going to be doing a house call then naturally the full address, including postcode, will be required. If it's a flat, then you're best asking about access, especially if you have a health condition yourself. (Think of carrying your therapy bed up flights of stairs.) Check that there will be room to set up your couch and that a plug socket is available if you'll need it to play your music, though you may wish to use tracks supplied by your client – see section about music licenses. It's also time to discuss whether the room allocated to the treatment will be able to offer the level of serenity you would like – unaffected by pets, phone calls, postal deliveries, infants etc.

I paid one house visit to a woman who said her pets would be no issue whatsoever. She owned a cat and a dog, and she stated they would both settle down perfectly well once we'd started. Both animals had either failed to hear this instruction, or were wilfully disobeying it. They proceeded to chase each other around her living room like some old-style cartoon, leading me to ask if perhaps we could place them in another room. The cat was shown the kitchen, but the dog was hastened out of the glass sliding doors that gave access to the garden. Unfortunately these doors afforded zero sound-proofing and therefore allowed every tone of his whining to reach us with perfect clarity. We continued for a further ten minutes, until it was obvious that his banishment was no precursor to silence. Indeed it was having completely the opposite effect. This dog wanted attention, and if he couldn't have it from the cat, then his owner had better make other arrangements.

The sliding doors were duly opened and my client claimed that since the cat had been evacuated from the room, and he was now back in with us, the dog would sit quietly and all would be calm. Only the dog was wanting to know what on earth his owner was doing lying on top of some sort of table. What would the view be like from that elevated position? Guess there's only one way to find out. So he did. By jumping up onto his owner and lying down on her stomach. And therefore also my blanket, which I take great pains to remain free of pet hairs in case any client has an allergy. If it had been a football match I think we'd have been looking at a score of dog six, tranquillity zero. Put it this way, the dog definitely won.

When deciding whether to work from your home, do consider the comings and goings of other people and animals in the house, and how this might impact a treatment. If you own pets, even if they are beautifully behaved and won't disturb a session, you may still need to raise this with any potential clients before they book an appointment with you. As just noted, do ensure that your couch covers, towels, and blankets remain free from pet hair, to avoid triggering allergic reactions.

Think through if you can offer suitable toilet facilities, because it won't be appropriate to tell your client they'll have to wait because your son is unexpectedly still in the bath.

Carry out a risk assessment of those areas that would be accessed by clients, to ensure you minimise the opportunity for accidents. Such as slipping on a rug, or tripping over wires etc.

As mentioned earlier, you will also need to ensure you comply with current legislation, local authority by-laws, home insurance clauses, and mortgage or rental agreements. Do also review your attitude towards both advertising your personal address, and accepting clients of the opposite sex.

When you are starting out, that last item is unlikely to be an issue if your appointment has been generated through somebody you know. However, when your business becomes more established and you begin accepting clients who have no connection with you, do use your intuition to filter out anyone who makes you feel uncomfortable.

If you receive a phone call or text from someone who, in any way, makes you question whether you wish to work with them, then don't. Your personal safety should never be compromised.

If you advertise working at several different venues, remember to confirm which site your client is intending to visit. Obvious, I know, but the obvious is much less so when you are unused to thinking about it, and in the excitement of those early requests for your services, you may not think about qualifying this information until after you have put the phone down.

Parking

Whether you are going to them, or vice versa, it's a good idea to mention parking. If the former, then you will need to know how easy and near to their home you can park. If the latter, then it is a way of easing the amount of stress that they will be under when they arrive. Better to be up front with them that parking can be a nightmare. At least then they will allow extra time and that will avoid adding any pressure, that during the appointment you'll be working hard to release.

If they live in an area with parking restrictions, you may need change to feed a meter, or to borrow their visitor's parking permit. You don't want to be worrying about such issues five minutes before you are due to be there.

Payment

Make clear at the time of booking what the fee will be. This ensures that there is a clear agreement between you.

If you don't have access to a credit card/debit card machine, it will be very worthwhile stipulating up front that you only accept cash or cheques, as appropriate. In an age that rarely uses either, it can simply not occur to somebody that they need to organise their method of payment in advance.

It's also a good policy to have a range of change available on the day itself, so remember to have a few lower denomination notes and coins to hand.

Should you decide to accept electronic payments, then you could consider either setting up a PayPal account, or use a mobile credit/debit card reader such as offered by SumUp or Square, for whom I have read positive reviews from other therapists.

Length of the Appointment

It is a good idea to mention the length of the sessions you provide, ensuring client's allocate themselves sufficient time. If you offer both one hour and ninety minute options you'll need to qualify which is relevant for each booking. Clarity of communication in all that you do really does pay dividends.

Now I am sure that you are a friendly person, but if shyness sometimes masks this, realise that building rapport is an important part of the job. As the Practitioner, you need to take the lead.

Putting the time and effort into building rapport from the outset, means new clients will be far more relaxed in your company by the time you meet. This in turn assists both the consultation and treatment stages. They'll be more likely to open up to you, and closing their eyes and surrendering to the Reiki will become less of a challenge. So make all communication friendly and caring from the outset, even where it makes you feel under pressure – whether through lack of confidence or time – and your natural inclination would be to simply provide the facts. More than once people have told me that they felt happy coming to see me because we'd built a relationship right from the start.

To assist this process it can be helpful to look at how your behaviour will come across from their perspective rather than your own. Although a few years ago now, an example really sticks in my mind when I shared a client with another therapist working in the same building as I did. This particular client (let's call her Fiona) had booked to try two differing styles of treatment in the same week. Mine was the second. I was genuinely surprised when she commented very negatively about the first. Apparently there had been no conversation or pleasantries exchanged, on the walk between the Reception and the therapy room.

Knowing the other therapist as being very personable (as well as skilled – I would happily recommend her to anyone), I can only assume that it was either an 'off' day for her, or that she leads her clients quietly to her therapy room, so as not to disturb others. Either way it had been poorly received by Fiona, who let me know that she wouldn't be returning to the other therapist for further treatments.

Create rapport at every opportunity.

Please note however, that you may need to amend your usual small talk, to remain appropriate within a therapy context. It didn't take me long to realise that when I come out with an automatic *"how are you?"* through polite convention, it's a completely unsuitable question until you are sitting down face to face. If it comes out unbidden, before you've reached the privacy of the therapy room, then any genuine response would break that most precious commodity between you – confidentiality. It then becomes more of a glib statement than a true question (empty words), and is not the basis for building a good relationship.

Even if you are working in your own home and shared space is not an issue, it is still effectively a health question. It should be asked when you can offer your full attention to the reply, and possibly have access to your notes, in case what is said needs to be recorded.

Whilst it might sound a little unimaginative, it truly is best to greet people with conversation about things like the weather, or if they could park easily. These are subjects that you can both be comfortable with, and are acceptable for one of you to be addressing the back of the other, as you walk to the treatment room.

Watch out for the minefield of the *"how are you?"* question when you receive a phone call from someone whom you have treated before. They may be calling you from work, surrounded by others, or maybe it just isn't fitting to have to field such a question when so much is going on for them that they need an appointment. My way round it has been to replace it with *"Oh ____, how lovely to hear from you."* This will then a) still be true and b) avoid any incongruity.

The final action in making a client booking, is a pre-treatment text or email reminder. Sending out a message the day before the treatment is scheduled really pays dividends by avoiding 'no-shows'.

To complete the appointment cycle, I like to text the client the day after their first treatment, to check up on how they are feeling. Not only does this allow me to show them I care but also, if they have experienced any type of healing reaction, it will give me the opportunity to put their mind at rest, and offer explanation. (As mentioned earlier, the new data protection legislation has led me to seek approval for such contact in advance. I now have a tick box on my Client Record which confirms that I have their permission.)

Marketing

Friends and family will get you only so far. If you're looking to make a business out of being a Reiki Practitioner (even on a part-time basis), you're going to need to advertise your services.

How fortunate that we live in an age where it is easy to produce marketing materials that look both appealing and professional. If you can afford to pay someone to help you, then great. However, if you are someone who is working on a tight budget, then please be assured that you can work solo with some basic keyboard skills.

It is good to think of yourself as a brand – to have continuity across your marketing media, with a logo or image, or at least a colour palette, by which you will be recognised quickly and easily.

However one of the worst things at this time is to allow any perfectionist tendencies to come out, because this is likely to cause procrastination. This reminds me of a woman I knew who was more than capable of being both a therapist and of putting together a decent leaflet. She agonised over the wording and layout so much that she never actually got anything printed. I did try to get across to her that just having something out there, was a good start. This is an example of where we unexpectedly come up against our own demons, and unfortunately they can put significant roadblocks in our path.

We all have to push through our comfort zone. Don't believe that because someone else has produced something, that it came naturally or easily to them. They are likely to have experienced all the self-doubt and inadequacies that you are experiencing; it's simply they have continued on anyway.

That was certainly my experience. I was fortunate enough to be asked to work at the therapy centre in which I trained, immediately after receiving my Reiki Master certificate. There was therefore immense pressure on me to produce a leaflet and a business card in double-quick time. It was not so much for myself, but rather so I didn't let the owner of the centre (and therefore also my Reiki teacher) down. Perhaps this worked in my favour. I couldn't delay or talk myself out of it. Something had to be put together and that was that.

In those days, most people self-printed their leaflets, and there are still some great advantages in doing so. I have amended my wording quite regularly, and changes to my pricing and venue have also required re-prints. There's a balance to be struck – potential benefits in quality if you outsource to a printing company, yet flexibility and cost savings if you keep it in-house.

I have always chosen to have my business card professionally printed. Its first incarnation led to major over-ordering. The combination of reduced rates pro-rata for volume, together with the lure of saving multiple postage costs, were coupled with a naive over-enthusiasm for believing I'd be handing them out left, right and centre. Many met their end in the paper recycling collection when I finally decided on my logo and they instantly became obsolete. There were far fewer opportunities to give them out than I had anticipated or common sense should have calculated. But then, it's a learning process.

Do yourself a favour and just start. You already know the main details:

- Your name.
- Job title – Reiki Practitioner or Reiki Master Practitioner. (If you've trained to Second Degree level, consider that you may well go on to become a Master. Your first business card may therefore have a short shelf-life. This is true too if you're thinking of setting up a website, because you'll want to add the web address as soon as possible.)
- Your telephone number.
- Email address.

That's it. Yes, really, that is all you need to begin advertising yourself. And I am guessing that you could write those down right now without even having to think about them. You may still want to consider a colour (background or text), a font and layout. But essentially you already know all you need to get started, particularly as it is perfectly acceptable to change your mind.

If your favourite colour is blue and that feels the way to go initially, but down the road you realise that green better expresses your services, then go green. Don't be hard on yourself and think that if it isn't exactly right, then it isn't good enough at all. Yes you want to love it, and know you resonate with it on some deep level. But you can find your way to that. Otherwise it is just too easy to make lack of perfection into an excuse for inertia.

Online companies such as Vistaprint can be very useful, as they will allow you to print your own design. Choose a template to which you can simply add your details. Or even ask one of their team's designers to create what you're looking for (I understand they are extremely helpful). If you are using someone else's image(s) then make sure you have copyright.

Once printed it's worth approaching some local shops and cafés in your area to see if they would kindly agree to stocking your leaflets, or might pin your business card to their noticeboard.

Most clients these days, however, find their therapist by searching online. If you haven't set up your own website yet, then there are a range of online therapist directory websites that you can join, mostly for free. These would give you Internet presence.

Think carefully about committing yourself to a fee for such services, as I would question whether your outlay would be re-paid. Whilst appreciating that my experience may not be yours, do note that your aim is to generate local interest in a specific healing method. You need to ask yourself if the enticing numbers of leads a company is quoting are country-based and across a large range of therapies. It might not equate to high numbers of enquiries specifically for Reiki and in your local town.

To find relevant directories simply do your own Internet search as if you were looking for a Practitioner. You can then select to advertise your services on any sites to which you are attracted. Additionally when you have set up your own website, you will be able to add the link to your directory entries, to tie them together.

Creating your own website may sound daunting but it really needn't be. Many of my friends have paid for a web designer or used someone they know with the relevant knowledge. This is obviously a great option. However I am living proof that you can set up and maintain your own website with IT skills honed only from using the likes of Word and Excel. There are a range of very good and easy-to-use packages out there. Ask around anyone you know that can give you a personal recommendation because then, even if they can't get involved in the whole process, you'll have someone to ask for help if you really get stuck.

The package I use is called BlueVoda, produced by VodaHost (www.vodahost.com). It is an American company that happily just showed up on a Google search many years ago. Their software has proven to be very straightforward to use, and, as their name suggests, they 'host' (support the publication of my website pages on to the Internet) too.

Do use your own words when you are writing your marketing material. In doing so you will encapsulate something of your own style, and this will help you to attract clients that are a good fit with your energy. You might want to look at a few examples from other people first, so that the blank white page you're faced with doesn't overwhelm you, but ultimately the benefit of expressing things your way will pay dividends.

It will also mean that you come more from your heart, and as a heart-centred business, what could be more appropriate? This can be where it is helpful to start simple. It took a while to express myself fully and know what I wanted to say. If this is how you are feeling, then start with the key details and expand from there in the future.

As long as you have the following, then you've covered the main things and provided enough for someone to get in touch with you:

- ❖ Everything I've already mentioned in relation to your business card/leaflet. (And make sure you add your website address to these as soon as it's operational).
- ❖ Venue (If you are working from home and you don't want to list your full address before you have vetted people, then you can always just name the village, town or city area, as appropriate).
- ❖ Price.
- ❖ Length of appointments. And you might also want to include the specific days and times you intend to offer treatments.
- ❖ Membership of any professional organisation.
- ❖ Special offers or reduced rates in particular circumstances. For instance I reduce my rates for Carers, give a free greetings card for pre-payment of a treatment when it is purchased as a gift, and have, in the past, provided discounts if a client pays for a series of three treatments in advance.

In the UK and European Union, (please check locally if you work outside of these regions), there is a requirement to adhere to legislation protecting the privacy of visitors to your website. Two aspects of this will require some action on your part. One relates to 'cookies', the second to clearly advertising your 'Privacy Policy'. Before your eyes roll skywards, unless you are gathering client data via your website, the implications require only minor adaptations which I'm sure you will be able to handle easily.

A cookie is a small text file that a website saves on your computer or mobile device when you visit the site. It enables the website to remember your actions and preferences (such as login, language, font size and other display preferences) over a period of time, so you don't have to keep re-entering them whenever you come back to the site, or browse from one page to another.

Now you may not believe this is relevant to you and the site you have created, but it is more than likely that the company that hosts your website is using them, and so anyone looking at your website will be affected. Legally it is your responsibility to make your users aware of this, and to inform them of what they are, and how they can be rejected.

You may well have noticed the (annoying) box that appears regularly now as you browse the Internet, specifying that "*this site uses cookies to ensure you get the best experience on our website*" or similar. It asks you to click both for your acknowledgement and permission to continue. Those websites are abiding by this legal requirement.

The good news is that there are some lovely people in this world. Some, like you, drawn to helping others. A bunch of them run a company called Silktide Ltd. providing you with a very simple way to make a similar cookie message box appear on your website. This can be linked to either your own, or a general Cookie Policy Statement. (If you visit your host's website, you'll be able to read their cookie policy and replicate the details.)

There is no charge whatsoever for this service – they don't even ask you to sign up or register. Just go to https://www.cookieconsent.insites.com. Click on the *'Download'* button, and follow the instructions. Perfect.

The second requirement is for your website to specify its 'Privacy Policy'. Again, this is a pretty straightforward requirement, unless you choose to gather client information from your website, such as when you ask potential clients to enter their details online using some kind of web form. If that's the case you will need to ensure your Privacy Policy reflects this, and investigate if you need to register with the Information Commissioner's Office (ICO) if in the UK.

However for those of us who are just advertising our existence via the web, it's a much easier process. You will simply need to make sure you build an additional webpage clearly stating your policy, and set up a highly visible link to it from your main (index) page.

Below is a list of the key sections of my Privacy Policy, which I hope provides you with some guidelines. As ever though, you need to satisfy yourself that you have met your legal obligations. Always therefore make the appropriate investigations to ensure you comply with all current legislation.

My privacy policy includes:

- ❖ Visitor consent for using my website.
- ❖ My contact details (email address).
- ❖ My right to amend the policy.
- ❖ The date from which it became active.

- ❖ For those people who are specifically seeking to arrange a treatment with me, an Informed Consent Agreement together with Data Protection Acknowledgements.
- ❖ A repeat of my Cookie Policy Statement.
- ❖ The details of web traffic analysis used by Google Analytics (Google Inc.) and the company that hosts my website, together with links to the Privacy Policies of both companies.

  If it seems a little over-whelming, then my advice is to read a few policies on other people's websites, so you get the gist of what is required. I'm sure you will surprise yourself at how easy it is to put your own policy together after having done so.

Where you are employed as a therapist in either England or Wales, there is a possibility that your employer will want to arrange for a DBS (Disclosure and Barring Service) check. If you work for yourself it isn't relevant, as only an employer can request this certification. A DBS check establishes if a person has any form of criminal record that would make them unsuitable for working with children or vulnerable adults. Should you possess a current DBS certificate, or if you are based in a country with a comparable vetting procedure, it's worthwhile highlighting this in your marketing documentation.

Make sure you stay within any legal constraints set by your country's advertising standards. In the UK for instance, advertising standards require that you don't make misleading or unsupportable claims. This means the avoidance of terms such as *"Reiki heals"* or *"Reiki will ..."*

Instead it is advisable to say *"Reiki **may**..."* (help you to reduce stress for instance).

Regarding the design side of things, it's best to pick a font that offers clarity across a variety of platforms. Initially using 'Papyrus' as my chosen font looked lovely on a leaflet, but didn't print particularly well on my business card, and looked very poor visually on my website. Remember too that these days the latter also has to be clear when viewed small-scale via a mobile phone. People are less likely to be reading your website on a large computer screen and you need to accommodate this. Wanting continuity as part of my branding meant I ended up changing my business card and leaflet again, simply to reflect the clearer typeface I eventually chose for my website.

Whatever choices you make regarding any written material, the happiest way to generate new clients is likely to be through recommendations. It always gives me a warm glowing feeling inside when it happens, and it can often be via a client I perhaps treated only the once! You think they haven't returned because they didn't get enough out of it, only to find that they have suggested their friend visits you four months down the road. So stay upbeat, even if it *seems* endorsements are not happening for you.

Get out there and start taking actions that may lead to appointments in your diary. As well as mentioning it wherever appropriate, consider offering your services at school pamper nights, or maybe a free treatment as a prize in a local raffle, at a summer fête or Christmas fayre. Establish a social media presence. Set up a Facebook business page, and generally just create opportunities by being inventive where you can.

Challenges As You Progress

When Appointments Don't Go As Expected (Small Things)

Having begun to advertise your services, you will be greatly increasing the opportunity for appointments to come your way. Whilst most appointments are pretty straightforward, and will follow a familiar format, there are also going to be times when this proves not to be the case. At the beginning, even minor adjustments to the norm can throw you a bit. Take heart though, because these will be the times when you will be able to notice your skills developing and your expertise growing.

But as they say *"forewarned is forearmed"* so let me share a few possibilities, along with how to cope with them…

The client cries

It is not uncommon for a recipient of Reiki to release tears. Often this is a gentle release where a tear or two will simply roll down their face, but it can result in a need to have a good old cry. I use my words deliberately. It is, in my estimation, a great benefit when this occurs, so do see it as a *good thing*.

It can be quite a shock however, if you never had this happen when you trained. And the speed at which it can arise can be startling. I recall it happening once when I had got all of about forty five seconds into a treatment.

I was looking to expand my business and had seen adverts asking for therapists interested in working in therapy rooms based at a pharmacy. Its location was a drive of about thirty minutes from where I lived and almost an hour's distance from my existing venue. Its site meant that it would not compete with my main work location, and when I introduced myself to the Manager she was exactly the type of person I would choose to work with. Very professional and motivated, mixed with kindness and a sense of humour. Her enthusiasm meant it was an easy decision to agree to advertise my services there.

The thought of Reiki operating in such an orthodox medical setting was actually part of the appeal. How amazing would it be to have someone pick up their prescription from the counter and then wander on through for a Reiki session? How many people could I introduce to the concept of complementary and more specifically energy therapy?

Contracts were signed, and the Manager agreed for me to offer her staff a free mini treatment. It is worth considering making a similar offer at any new venue where you provide your services. Not only is it a lovely good-will gesture, but also it will enable receptionists to have some idea of what Reiki would feel like for anyone making enquiries about your service.

When it came to the Manager's turn, she had been lying down for a matter of moments, my hands hovering above her head, and the tears fell.

She was embarrassed. She shared with me that she was someone who never showed their vulnerability. The consummate professional. And here she was crying in front of someone with whom she was to have a working relationship. The power of Reiki energy is truly amazing. Such an effect within seconds.

Now I was well enough into my career at this point to be comfortable with the experience. It was only the rate at which it happened that caught me unawares. The first incidence of crying, however, had me completely unprepared. As I recall there was no mention of the possibility at my training, and during it no one had responded in that way.

When it is just the silent release of a tear, it can be hard to assess whether to interrupt the quietness of the treatment to ask if a tissue would be appropriate. Use your intuition and feel the answer.

If you do choose to ask the question, softly whisper it, so that you don't shock your client out of their emotional state. Beginning a sentence with the word "and" is a calm introduction, so you may like to try saying in hushed tones something along the lines of *"and if you would like a tissue then gently nod your head"* – providing a response that doesn't require speech can also help to elicit an answer without too great an interruption into what is obviously a deeply emotional (healing) experience.

If the crying is more obvious then you might want simply to offer a tissue and provide some words of comfort and support, confirming the release of tears is simply a (very visible) form of letting go and therefore incredibly beneficial to the healing process.

Frequently clients will have no idea what has prompted them to cry. In my experience there is absolutely no requirement for them to do so. We do not need to analyse or make conscious all of the processing that is being performed at an unconscious level. If they do know and choose to share the reason then that's fine but if they don't then that's fine too. The important thing is that they realise the therapeutic significance of what has happened.

And tears may fall for a number of reasons, including the beauty of being touched compassionately by another human being, feeling an unconditionally loving energy, or as an expression of grief or loss that has long been suppressed.

So welcome the tears; they are healing. Let your clients be confident that they are a natural part of the process. Hold space for them whilst it happens. By this I mean imagine your energy gently supporting and holding them in a strong yet compassionate way.

Also, don't be surprised if the tears come to you. Occasionally they will simply begin rolling down my face during a treatment and I know that I am releasing them on behalf of the client. In my case they arrive without introduction – there is usually no imagery or emotional upsurge to prompt them, they simply begin to fall.

Accordingly it's good to always have a box of tissues on hand; no Reiki room is complete without them.

And for women affected by post-tear mascara runs or similar, I have found it to be kinder to point out the issue rather than stay quiet.

A mirror can be a good addition to your therapy venue.

The client falls asleep

Unlikely to have happened whilst you were training, but be prepared for this to happen in the future.

It is not unusual for my clients to fall asleep during a treatment and so far I am encouraged that this has only occurred once they are on the therapy couch.

A proportion of such clients may snore and so it appears that they are in a deep sleep. However, my advice is to always continue as if they are still awake, because many will be drifting in and out of varying levels of consciousness. There have been occasions when I thought a client fully out for the count for the whole duration, only for them to subsequently tell me that they had a particular response when I moved to a certain part of their body.

Naturally Reiki works equally well whatever state of awareness the recipient is experiencing. Whilst it can be an advantage for a client to remain sufficiently alert to acknowledge their body's feedback, allowing their mind to recognise that they are actively responding to the energy, their being in a less conscious state does allow the Reiki to work without hindrance, doubt or negative self-talk. Here we have complete surrender and therefore an acceptance to receive – removing any attempts to block or control. This can be very powerful.

I like to suggest that a client allows themselves to respond as their body is leading them and that if that means sleep, just to go with it, with the advantages mentioned above.

In instances where a client is very keen to stay awake and enjoy the experience but usually drifts off, it can be helpful to place a suggestion at the beginning of the session. When they are lying down and beginning to relax, I may say something like *"and the more relaxed you become, the more aware you are"*. We don't want their willingness to remain alert to prevent them from letting go of tension or stress. Invite their mind to calm whilst their focus heightens to any sensations.

This provides the client with an opportunity to move into a state of simply 'being' – alert only to the gifts brought by their mind being attentive to the present moment.

The client can't lie in a 'typical' position

I usually work with people lying down on their back on a therapy couch. It seems so minor for someone to say that doesn't suit them, but actually, the first time that it occurred I found it quite a surprise. You may find that they wish to lie face down (I know some of you will have been trained to execute half of the treatment in this way but others, like me, will find this unusual), and I have had several who choose to lie on their side – so all those standard hand positions are out of reach.

As I mentioned earlier, I wasn't instructed on particular positions to use during a treatment, but have noticed how certain places on the body generally feel good places to be, such as either side of the head (ah, she's on her side, that won't work); above both armpits (ah, can only reach one of those). It is amazing how familiarity for us humans makes us feel comfortable, and change can therefore be a challenge. Just be prepared for such circumstances and you will find you can then easily go with the flow. And of course one of the benefits that Reiki has over other therapies, is that you can work off the body and so you don't need to reach any particular point on it at all.

You may find advantages in letting the client know before you start, that it's fine for them to move during a treatment. At times when I have forgotten to mention this in advance, I've noticed how some people are so keen to please others (and their Reiki Practitioners) that they will lie rigid as if in a straight-jacket, so they don't do anything 'wrong'.

But of course, firstly we want the recipient to be as comfortable as possible. So if they need to move an arm or a leg, then we should be pleased they do so. And secondly, I've found (particularly as my Reiki has developed,) that more and more often, the bodies of my clients will naturally twitch and flex as parts of their body release trauma or emotion, or sometimes as a way of re-balancing and re-aligning itself. So it can be a real plus to give your clients permission to respond freely within the treatment so that they get the most out of it.

Of course it may be that someone simply needs to scratch their nose and it would be so much better if they did so and got it out of the way so they can relax back into the treatment, rather than wondering whether they are *allowed* to do so. Remember that whilst your aim is to empower your client, many will see you as the one controlling the session. It's easy for the less self-assured to assume that they should do nothing they have not been given express permission to do.

Which reminds me of my first introduction to energy healing some years before I found Reiki, through a friend who unfortunately drifted out of my life very soon afterwards. I had been working in London for many years for a company called Reuters and towards the end of my time there, I made friends with a colleague – a very lovely woman named Emma. As our time together was nearing its end Emma took a course in a form of energy therapy and she offered me a session. Intrigued, I naturally accepted.

She asked me to stand in the middle of her living room, with my eyes closed as she worked the energy around me. I could feel my energy being pulled and pushed. My body wanted to sway with that motion, but for quite some time I resisted doing so because I didn't know that was what was meant to happen! After a while, the impulse was too strong and I began to allow myself to gently circulate my body with the current, whilst keeping my feet firmly in one position on the floor. It felt amazing.

Afterwards, Emma had said how pleased she was to have seen me going with the energy because a man she had recently done a session for had stood rock solid in the room and she had felt exasperated by the whole experience.

But perhaps he felt he was doing what he was *supposed* to do?

Always remember that people can't second guess or mind-read what is meant to be happening because there is nothing in our everyday way of living that can act as the instruction manual for such situations. A person's nearest equivalent is likely to be a doctor's surgery where you are usually expected to stay still unless instructed to move in a specific way.

One word of advice to the inexperienced, though, about the physical positions in which to run a treatment, is that I will now only carry them out where the recipient is either lying down or seated. My training, however, suggested that the best position for working on people's backs was to have them standing with their hands resting for support on the couch, the back of a chair or similar.

Part of the reasoning behind this was that this position allowed for the back to re-adjust itself more easily and I can provide you with examples of where it has attained very successful results. All great until one day when I was treating a man who fainted during his treatment. He said that I just moved my hands to a particular position and it felt like almost an electric shock went through him and he passed out.

He came round within a few seconds, but by that time he was on the floor and being tall in stature it had been quite a drop. I called an ambulance.

The paramedic asked to speak to him directly as he was up and in a chair by the time I had placed the call. There was going to be quite a delay for them to attend so for the next forty minutes I was left to 'chat' as we waited. I can't tell you how dreadful I felt. It was so awful to seemingly achieve the exact opposite of what I had been hoping for and in such an incredibly dramatic way.

After the forty minutes, the ambulance service rang me back and asked once again to speak to my client who assured them that he didn't require any help and so the call-out was duly cancelled. Naturally I offered to drive my client to his home but he was adamant that he was fine and could make his own way there.

All I could do was feel awful all evening, phone him in the morning to check he was still alright and to suggest that he visit his GP in case there was an issue. Mercifully, he was fine but the thought of endangering someone when you are focused purely on helping them was incredibly sobering. No, not sobering, down-right terrifying.

Actually the shock of it all made me feel awful for a lot longer than over-night and it made me review how to handle back treatments. Nowadays if I feel it is right to place my hands directly onto someone's back then they will be lying either face down or on their side on the therapy couch, or sitting on a chair. Of course Reiki doesn't require any of these options. Often I will continue to have a client remain lying on their back through the whole treatment knowing the Reiki can go to their spine without direct contact if I intend it, or imagine my hands being placed there.

Which leads me to suggest you mention to a client in your pre-treatment consultation, that it is not always necessary for you to be touching or working over the point of injury or physical trauma of their body, in order for it to heal. It is interesting to note that many people will imagine that you have to be working on their knee if issues with the knee are what has brought them to you in the first place.

Because your recipient will be healing themselves, you want to avoid creating any block to this by placing doubt or disquiet in their mind. If they are lying there thinking, *"I explicitly told her that I have an issue with my shoulder so why on earth is she spending all this time at my ankles?"* that is not going to help them trust the process. You might therefore consider a brief explanation that will assist your clients in their understanding. This might include your relationship with chakras (energy centres), your intuition, or how auric scanning (where you feel your way in the energy around an individual's body) will be guiding you to where the Reiki energy is best accepted. This may or may not relate directly to the consciously known point of imbalance.

Don't worry if you forget though, because you will likely just be told at the end of the appointment that they were feeling so many sensations in the relevant part of their body that they will have reached this conclusion themselves anyway.

I've already mentioned that I'll treat some clients whilst they remain seated, such as at times when I am drawn to lay my hands directly on their back, but naturally it may also become appropriate for clients if they are in a wheelchair. It's worth noting that I have had recipients drift into beautiful semi-conscious states even whilst sitting bolt-upright on the most unforgiving of wooden seats, so be assured that this is no barrier to a receiving a wonderful Reiki experience.

There is the likelihood of noise during a treatment, or an unexpected noise occurs

During my time I have worked in a range of unlikely settings which are a world away from the idyllic oasis of calm that one might traditionally wish for. These include pubs (a friend mentions that they have an issue with their right arm and I can therefore let the Reiki flow whilst sitting next to them, chatting over a pint, well actually more likely wine but you get the point), and pamper evenings at schools where you think you'll be allocated a quiet space only to find that the therapy beds are all at one end of the main hall and at 9:30pm the head of the Parent Teacher Association is going to be calling out the winning raffle ticket numbers over the microphone.

At the centre where I now base my clinic, they occasionally hold Open Days. These include offering taster treatments to showcase the range of therapies we provide. They tend to take place in a cacophony of sound. One year there were eight therapy couches in one room, running twenty minute sessions, so there was a constant coming and going of the next-booked recipient. Trails of people coming either to have a look at what was going on, or to book themselves in for their 2:20pm Shiatsu.

The day was hot, so windows were open, but this led to our gentle therapy music having to compete with the pop music beats being played at the café. There were constant sounds of talking, and laughter both in and outside of the room and yet I still had some Reiki recipients switch off completely.

One particular gentleman who was experiencing his first introduction to Reiki was in his late seventies or early eighties. He had been devastated by the recent death of his wife, whom he had been lovingly caring for over the last few years.

Amongst all the activity of the event, he told me as he got down from the couch, that he had been transported into a series of holiday scenes with his wife. It was just as if he were back with her in the beauty of the nature that they had so enjoyed together when they were younger. He asked me if the room had been emptied for his twenty minutes, so complete was his connection to those times.

There will be others who find it horribly distracting to have anything but near perfect silence, but I suggest to them that that is rarely available to any of us, even in our own homes. How much better to be able to feel peace even in the midst of sound? To sense the peace *within* no matter what is happening around us. And I'll raise this point whenever I'm going to be giving Reiki in circumstances where there will be some distractions that might affect a client. For instance, it is usual for me to say, as we begin the Reiki, something along the lines of *"and the sounds you hear, whilst you are here, remind you that this is a safe place to relax and let go, and you can **choose** to make every sound deepen this relaxing experience further"*.

In doing so I have given them a way of handling what might be a negative, in a positive way that can add to the treatment. This also means that it is easier to relax as the therapist, because you don't cringe every time you hear something – you are allowing sounds to lead you deeper. Also providing the appearance of choice whilst delivering an instruction is a way of more readily gaining agreement to accept that instruction. Most of us don't like being told what to do, even when it is to our advantage, so offering (perceived) choice can be a way of overcoming that form of resistance.

Note also how 'sounds' are easier to have a positive relationship with than 'noises' – every word you use can play its part in a treatment.

You may like to note that one of my clients who was extremely sensitive to any sound always brought ear plugs with her so, as listed earlier, this might be another idea to bear in mind.

Where there is a sudden and unexpected loud and obtrusive sound it can help to acknowledge it as it happens. I sometimes use it as a light-hearted confirmation of healing taking place. For example a workman's drill suddenly beginning might lead me to say *"and the Reiki energy is now drilling down into every cell and atom of your body"* or *"and you can notice how you are drilling away the old beliefs and patterns of behaviour that no longer serve you"*.

Remember also that you are sharing energy with your client, and so how *you* are reacting to noises can have a direct impact on how they respond. If you are in a state of calm or humorous acceptance, this will assist your client to be as well.

The first venue I worked from after my training was, as I mentioned earlier, the healing centre which my Reiki teacher owned. I think it was only my third time of working there when I found myself serenaded by a Town Crier.

I was still so much rabbit-in-the-headlights-new to being a therapist that when, about twenty minutes in to a beautifully peaceful Reiki session, I was hearing *"oh yay, oh yay, up to 50% off at the Hawkins sale today"* accompanied by a loudly rung bell, you can imagine how toe-curling I found it. It was like my inner joy visibly shrivelled into a small ball of pure embarrassment. There was nothing I could do about it. The windows were already closed, and I would have had to turn my music up to a non-existent volume twenty five to have had any chance of drowning out the intrusion.

All I could do was laugh and apologise. To be honest it wasn't a very honest laugh. I was too mortified to find any real humour in the situation. However, it did establish the efficacy of openly acknowledging what is happening and then proceeding to make the best of things.

Clients are usually far more understanding than you are likely to give them credit for.

The second venue in which I worked, was a gym based in my local town. It was, and indeed still is, a large-scale establishment and downstairs they housed two therapy rooms, hired out at very reasonable rates.

My client base was still far too erratic (and I must confess continues to be) to merit hiring a room by monthly contract. I required somewhere that I could pay for as and when appointments came my way.

The rooms were rather small and no frills, but I was delighted with the opportunity to work there. The lower floor additionally housed a spa area with hot tub and sauna, changing rooms and toilets and a room that didn't appear to be used for anything. That is until one evening when I was in the middle of a Reiki treatment, which began to be interrupted by the sound of people's voices chatting as a nearby door opened and closed with monotonous regularity.

You know the volume twenty five that was missing from *my* CD player? Found it.

The room had been transformed into a Spin Class. For the uninitiated, this is where a collection of static exercise bikes are pedalled for the most part with great ferocity, to the accompaniment of 'banging tunes' and a trainer who motivates the activity by shouting. Well you'd need to be shouting to be heard over the music wouldn't you? Reiki session abandoned; no payment accepted.

Over the years I have made improvements in my ability to work in less than perfect conditions, but know I would still be happiest if I could create a faultless environment.

Life's lessons continue.

When Appointments Don't Go As Expected (Some Bigger Things)

In addition to those situations we have just discussed, there are some slightly more taxing reasons for appointments not going quite as you would usually expect. But don't worry – you'll handle them…

The client doesn't want to close their eyes

If you are anything like me, then part of the pleasure in receiving Reiki is to close your eyes and go into that beautiful state of deep relaxation. To drift, who knows where, and feel the freedom of going beyond the physical. However, not everyone finds themselves capable of letting go to the point where they can close their eyes and relax into a treatment. I have worked with a number of clients for whom it would cause them additional stress to do so. My aim (if they choose to continue Reiki sessions with me) will be to get them to the point where this changes, but day one, it is just not going to happen.

Whilst you might expect such fears to go hand-in-hand with someone who appears scared of everything, those people are usually timid and therefore so compliant that they will close their eyes without issue.

No, I'm mostly referring to those that come across as very strong and independent people, which hides an undercurrent of extreme anxiety. Their anxiety leads them to feel that they need to control as much as possible. Most often these clients find it comforting to talk through the treatment because talking is a form of control; whilst closing your eyes is surrender.

The good news is that I can assure you that your Reiki will not be impeded as a consequence, but if you are used to conducting your sessions in a serene peace, it can feel awkward when you first encounter an individual who looks at you wide eyed in terror simply at the thought of lying down with their eyes shut.

One woman for whom this was true, let's call her Anna, could not have seemed less likely to fit into this category. Here was a woman in her fifties who was competently running several businesses. Not small-scale solo projects either, she was heading up teams of staff, at several locations. On the face of it she seemed very astute and capable. Scratch beneath the surface however and she was crippled with anxiety, sabotaging both her personal and professional life.

Her initial description of her circumstances, which on later appointments revealed to be just the tip of the iceberg, was littered with words which denoted how scared and vulnerable she felt in every aspect of her experience. The bottom line was she was making herself hugely overly responsible for looking after everyone and everything in her life…except herself.

Ask Anna to create a business plan and then deliver on it – sorted. Ask Anna to lie down and relax – panic. She truly couldn't comprehend what that meant, so distant in her memory was any feeling that would come close to fit the expression.

Realising her distress, I knew that even lying down in someone else's company was an achievement and so we ran the treatment with her fully alert and in conversation. I was even unable to ask her to take the three slower, deeper breaths which I usually prescribe to settle a client when they first lay down on the couch. This was because the main reason she had contacted me was to overcome her continued anxiety regarding her breathing and she had already told me at the consultation stage, that focusing on her breath scares her. Anna had been checked over several times by various members of the medical profession, all thankfully confirming nothing sinister, and yet Anna's mind had been unable to calm accordingly.

I had no idea whether we were going to be chatting about the weather and how there was never enough chocolate in the house when you needed it, or something more healing in nature.

The wonderful thing about setting your intention to serve and help someone to heal themselves as much as they are able, is that most times, that is exactly what happens and without you actively having to direct the proceedings.

Anna began to give herself her own wisdom. She raised issues that other people kept telling her that she had but that she couldn't see in herself, so she could (gently) see them in herself.

To be honest a part of me was feeling out of my depth – I am not a trained counsellor – however, when you are working in a Reiki environment, somehow you are led to respond at the right time and in the right way. Allow yourself to be guided. Trust.

As I held my hands about twenty centimetres above her torso, Anna told me she was feeling sensations as if a cat was padding on her stomach. Whenever I was over her ankles it apparently felt like a cool breeze was wafting over her feet. This is why I can say with conviction that talking through an appointment loses none of the magic or power. Believe.

Returning a week later, Anna reported that she felt her mind was now telling her that her health was settling down. The depth of despair that she had been feeling was not as deep as it had been. She had gone without taking her 'calm' tablets for a few days, excepting for the day she had returned to work (she'd been on a few weeks of sick leave for heightened anxiety when we met). Her grandchildren had bad colds and yet she had not worried that it would affect her chest. Fantastic!

After three appointments Anna was *telling me* how she need to *"let go"* and *"to love herself more"*. Fabulous. Don't you just love it when people give themselves their own good advice?

Major progress.

However there was a limit to how much she felt comfortable altering about herself in the short term, especially as she felt such changes would have significant repercussions on her family. She had just four sessions after which she texted me to explain and to put further treatments on hold for now.

Do remember that when people do not return for further treatments and you don't receive a comparable explanation, it may just be because your work was (well) done.

The client requires supervision

It may be that you are working with a child or young person, or perhaps with someone who has special needs.

There will be some practical considerations to make in advance of the appointment such as an extra glass of water, and to decide how you're going to seat an additional person in your treatment room. In the room where I work there are some chairs that are more solid and padded. Even if the parent has not been sitting in one for the initial consultation, I will guide them to sit there during the treatment, so that they are both more comfortable and on a chair that doesn't tip and swing, or creak too loudly if they become restless during the Reiki. Small things, but then they often make a difference to the ease with which a treatment goes.

Additionally, I ensure I have printed out a copy of a document to be signed by the legal guardian of the client concerned. There are legal guidelines in the UK affecting the treatments of those deemed to be children in the eyes of the law. And likely comparable requirements in whichever country you operate. In the UK you must make certain that you have the signature of a parent or guardian to authorise you to treat a minor.

I ask them to sign and date a typed document, using wording requested by the UK Reiki Federation, which specifies the following:

"A parent or guardian who wilfully fails to provide adequate medical aid for a child under the age of sixteen,

may be committing a criminal offence. Reiki is not defined as a medical aid by law, so anyone who treats a child whose parents refuse medical aid, could be seen to be aiding and abetting that offence.

I have been warned by Sarah Cooper that, according to Law, I must consult a doctor concerning the health of my child."

This is obviously to protect a child's health where orthodox medicine is clearly the correct route to take. If a child has difficulty breathing then they need to be at the A&E department of a hospital, not on a therapy couch with some softly playing music.

I also ensure it's understood that it's likely the Reiki will affect *all* those in the room, and not just the main recipient. Having had several parents who have been noticeably moved by the Reiki themselves, it has been reassuring to have made them aware upfront of the possibility that sensations and emotions may well make themselves known, even when they are sitting a meter or two from their child and therefore well away from what appears to be the direction in which the Reiki will go. This is another benefit of providing the sort of chair into which they can more easily relax, because they may be going in and out of that trance-like state that Reiki can create.

If it is a young child you'll definitely want the parent in the room with you, and anything else that might bring them comfort. I suggest to the parent that they bring a toy, particularly a soft toy that can be cuddled during the treatment. It can also be a great access point to receiving the child's feedback on how the session went – much less threatening to ask how the teddy bear felt.

When working with younger children I believe it is necessary for the parent or guardian to accompany the child during every treatment. Whereas with teenagers I am happy for a second appointment to run without chaperoning if this is requested and sought by both parties. I have often found that the young person will welcome this opportunity partly because they are now comfortable with what to expect, and partly because it may afford them the opportunity to share some of the reasons behind their stress or worries.

We'll look a little more fully at working with young people in a later chapter.

Anxiety strikes

I guess there aren't that many jobs in the world where it is appropriate to say, and really mean, you know your job well enough to be able to *"do it with your eyes closed"* but of course that is eminently possible in the world of Reiki. The downside can be that you miss certain signals that your recipient might be providing if you were looking directly at them. We've already discussed some beneficial signals in an earlier chapter, so now we need to consider where you may be in a beautifully colourful trance-like state, unaware of uneasiness arising in your client.

More than once I have been in a deliciously meditative oasis of calm when a client has told me that they are feeling the exact opposite. At the very point when my own awareness has been reduced to a vague acknowledgement that 'somewhere' my client must be floating in an equally comforting ... I have abruptly been pulled back into full alert consciousness by the words *"I'm sorry Sarah, I'm having a panic attack!"*

Hopefully just knowing it can happen will mean that you are not far from your best resources to deal with it and for you to realise that it is nothing that you are doing wrong, nor is it the Reiki failing.

It is also one of the reasons why it is so important to gain rapport with a client from the outset, as this ensures that they are more comfortable expressing what is happening for them, as and when it does so.

The first time it happened in my company it was to a man who I'll refer to as Steve. It was hard not to let my mind panic as much as his body obviously was, because you do ask yourself what on earth you can do when *everything* you are *currently* doing is aimed at reducing stress and inducing relaxation. To be frank I didn't know. On the outside I was just trying to be calm and professional; on the inside it was a complete big and rather shaky question mark.

Firstly it was obviously important to ascertain whether he wanted or was able, to continue. When he confirmed that he felt he could carry on, I asked him to take a few slower, deeper breaths and to let me know how he was feeling as the rest of the session progressed. Something told me it would be helpful to give his mind images that would divert his attention and so inwardly I asked to be given a sense of how the Reiki was flowing which would allow description.

In my mind's eye I could see that the energy was like a huge column of pale lilac light passing in through his head and cascading in ripples down through his body. As I shared the images with him, it seemed to calm him and direct his mind away from his fears. We got through to the end of the appointment time without further incident and pleasingly he did return on several occasions for more appointments. It made me wonder though, what else can be offered?

Nowadays I would therefore also suggest that you consider the following alternatives:

- ❖ *Guided Imagery* allows you to take a client's mind to a beautiful place so that they have something positive to focus on. Do be aware though, that the most innocuous of images to you can be stress triggers for someone else. So it is ***essential*** to ask them what type of environment is most restful to them before starting. You don't want to be describing a lovely beach scene if they have a phobia of water or they had a traumatic incident in their childhood that occurred on family trip to the seaside. So ask them where in nature they feel most drawn to. Because they are making the decision, this is also a way of empowering them. Many clients have said that they have gone on to re-visit the place they have created in their mind in their own time before sleep or when they are stressed. It is like a gift to themselves because they have built the bridge to it, with their inner wisdom giving them the answer of how to help themselves relax.

  It can be helpful to mention more than once that they are in a *safe* place and that the mind's eye environment they are taking themselves to, is completely safe and loving.

When working with the energy of images, it can also be helpful to know that individuals mostly respond in varying degrees to one of the three main senses of seeing, hearing and feeling (visual, audio and kinaesthetic). If you are working with a person who is very visual by nature, then painting pictures in their mind by describing say a garden scene with *"**bright colourful** flowers and lush **green** grass"*, is likely to be very appealing. However, if they are more audio responsive, then you will not be engaging them to any real degree until you introduce references to say *"**hearing** a bird **singing** in the trees" and "the **rustle** of the leaves"*.

Similarly, someone who is very feeling orientated, will most easily be led into the visualisation when you make references such as *"and you can feel the **warming** sun **gently touching** your face"* or *"you **feel calm** and **peaceful** as you walk on"*. My suggestion would therefore be to use elements that incorporate each sense (and you may like to include taste and smell also, although these tend to be of lesser importance to the majority of people), to ensure that you absorb them into the process as fully as possible.

Even if your client is in no way anxious, you may find incorporating descriptive scene-making an advantage on occasion. Thinking of one person in particular who attends my clinic every four to six months, this is certainly the case. When I met her for the second or third time, she told me that she was having real problems switching off and letting her mind go quiet. I suggested that we could try continuing whilst using the energy of relaxing images, and she readily agreed.

Afterwards she stated how this had allowed her to go beyond thoughts of what she was having for dinner and the To Do List for her business, and so the next time we met she requested that I gave her another scene in which to immerse herself. Over the years we've soared over landscapes like a bird on the wing, we've watched beautiful sunsets and floated in little boats peacefully down tree-lined rivers.

And if you are in anyway concerned that you are not a great story teller or that your powers of description will not be up to the job, be comforted by the fact that a person's imagination can be sparked by the merest of suggestions. You don't need huge detail and you can leave plenty of space in between one sentence and the next to allow for their unconscious mind to beautifully fill in the gaps. Also you'll likely find that after five or ten minutes, they are relaxing sufficiently that you can allow silence to take over.

Be assured that you are not trying to paint a complete scenario. Rather you are offering invitations for a person's own creativity to step forward. Hence you might speak of them standing on the top of a green hill whilst they experience being at the top of a mountain. The object is not for them to construct your vision in their heads, but to use it as a way of letting their own inner wisdom take them on a beautiful journey. Your only criteria is to ensure they know they are always safe and that only positive feelings will be generated as a consequence.

And do always remember to ask your client's permission to work in this way. Whilst images are so often an integral part of the Reiki experience, our aim is actually for them to come only naturally, as part of the process. Therefore employing it as a technique should only be used with discretion and for as little of the treatment as possible.

- ❖ *Keeping their eyes open all or most of the time*. Just let them know that this is perfectly acceptable. Also consider mentioning to all your clients that they are free to open their eyes at any point during a session. This is because I have noticed how failure to do so can lead recipients to attempt surreptitiously opening one eye to see where I am, whilst hoping that I won't notice. The implication being that they should be lying completely still with eyes tight shut the whole way through.

  Now part of my pleasure is to spread the wonder of Reiki and so to me, it is an added bonus when I know that someone feels compelled to look because that usually indicates they are having a moment of wonder all of their own. *"How can she possibly be working at my head and my feet at the same time???? Wow."*

  I don't want the magic of that moment tainted with thoughts that they are somehow doing the wrong thing, and thus giving them any cause to take on stress which we are investing so much in releasing.

- ❖ *Keeping their eyes open and having a conversation*. One such occasion really helped a young man to relax into the treatment. It wasn't anything that he said to me, but I knew I was simply being guided by a force wiser than myself to converse with him during the session.

His passion was in fantasy books and games and whilst this was an area which would be considered light to non-existent on my CV, we were able to have a decent chat about Lord of the Rings. The Reiki was particularly strong for him, so again do not concern yourself that you are providing any less of a service if you find yourself in similar circumstances. In fact you may well be able to help empower your client during the verbal exchange, thereby generating more healing opportunities whilst the Reiki just does its thing.

And remember Reiki doesn't require us to be all serious and earnest in our work. Laughter is another of the great healers in this world.

- *Sitting up and having a drink of water.* Sometimes just the opportunity of having a short break is highly beneficial.

- *Getting up completely and moving to a chair.* More recently a new client who came with a view to specifically releasing her anxiety, experienced the beginnings of a panic attack within about ten minutes or so of the Reiki commencing. Let's call her Olivia. The interesting thing was that this was on our second meeting, you'd think it more likely on the first wouldn't you? Indeed the week beforehand, I had been pleasantly surprised at how she had been able to close her eyes for most of the time and look calm and peaceful.
On that earlier occasion we had discussed, in the pre-treatment consultation, how she had been experiencing panic attacks and that she had been unable to link them

to any particular trigger. In fact she had felt that the only logical reason – that of immense stress created by intense work commitments – had been removed since she had been signed off from work for an extended period of time.

In my observation, if the original stressor (such as overwork) creates intense feelings around a lack of safety generated by thoughts of being out of control in a given situation, then the mind can endeavour to exert excessive control into *other* life situations providing it with the illusion of maximising its safety. This can also lead it to over-react through sensing a lack of control in even benign scenarios where ostensibly there should be no issue. The stress from such a perceived lack of control can present itself in an exceptionally diverse range of circumstances that have nothing to do with the original issue.

By its nature, relaxation is the opposite of control because it implies a level of surrender and letting go. Within a Reiki treatment the recipient is effectively required to relinquish control to the Practitioner. Anxiety can therefore be generated even *by* relaxation. The implication being that it's not safe for them to relax because then they are not in control.

However, if Reiki is a suitable methodology for guiding a particular individual back to a more appropriate sense of their own safety, then it is possible to witness wonderful transformation in this area.

One other reason as to why a client might experience anxiety *during* a treatment, is the possibility that Reiki is bringing to the surface feelings that have formerly been suppressed, but can now be released. It is often recognised amongst Practitioners that, at times, the site of an old physical trauma within the body of a recipient, can temporarily (re)generate feelings of pain or discomfort, as if the body was signalling it's letting go past injuries or imbalances. It may therefore be true too for emotional pain – an event primarily designed to allow a client to witness the letting go of *past* emotional states.

Back now though to Olivia, who had been perfectly able to cope with her first appointment and in the pre-treatment consultation on her second, had also appeared entirely at ease with the process. She explained how she had felt really well for the three to four days following her first session, but then had felt very low since then. I was able to confirm that this was very typical in my experience, and that as someone continues with a course of treatments, the positive results are maintained for longer and longer periods until hopefully the improvements become the new 'norm'.

Olivia then made her way onto the therapy couch and we began the Reiki until she explained that she was experiencing the beginnings of a panic attack. She could feel it welling up inside her. I asked her how she knows when it is happening and then how she knows when it is coming to a close. The latter was a deliberate way of eliciting a focus, however minor, on the symptoms ending. It also allowed us to confirm that Olivia was *safe* – she knew that the symptoms would stop. In such circumstances, where it's not a person's first experience of an attack, it can be beneficial to remind them that there will be a positive outcome. That after the sensations have peaked, they will then subside.

I brought Olivia some water and then asked if she would like to stop the session, or whether she felt she might be more comfortable sitting up for a while. Olivia told me how she would like to sit in a chair and once she was comfortably in hers, I took the one opposite explaining that I would gently continue with the Reiki at this new distance, unless she asked me to stop which she could do at any time. To ensure there was visual acknowledgement of what was occurring and nothing covert, I directed my hands slightly outwards and towards her.

The chair she was seated in was next to a very large floor-standing pot plant, beside a window and as her gaze connected with it, she noticeably calmed a little.

Intuitively I felt that she had a strong connection to plants and asking if this really was the case, Olivia was able to raise a smile as she told me of her garden and how she considers this her sanctuary. Although she had enjoyed many aspects of her career as an engineer, she wasn't missing the work now that she was on long-term sick leave and had found increasing pleasure just being in her garden at home.

As with many who are struggling with anxiety, and actually probably to some degree everyone whom I see as a Practitioner, Olivia was constantly in her head. Even when we were talking about feelings, Olivia would begin a sentence with *"I **think** I feel _____"*. There seemed to have somewhere been a disconnection from her heart and her true feelings and so I knew that moving her attention back to those was going to be an important part in her healing herself.

As we spoke of her garden I asked her whether she had some wish to change her career and work more in this field (pardon the pun). Olivia's response was *"it feels like my heart very much wants to but my head says no"*. The alarm bells rang, the sirens wailed. Here we are then. This is one of the areas of your life in which you are not daring to lead with your heart, and yet it is clearly trying to tell you of its passion. It is filling your body with signals – *feelings* – and yet in your mind-dominant world, its callings are being blotted out by your thoughts.

This is an excellent example of where the inner wisdom that we all have tends only to whisper, never shout.

We have to listen for the quiet voice that speaks from our heart, rather than the loud, shouty one that our head is all too familiar with. Because unfortunately, the heart rarely gets to yell from the rooftops making you feel like there is no way other than to embrace your passions. To my way of thinking it is because this quiet, almost imperceptible whisper is also coming from your Soul. But since the personality has ultimate freedom of choice, the Soul will only (very) softly beckon you forwards. Hence why, if you are constantly too much in your head, you can often fail to hear it – giving it little opportunity to speak up and pushing it away all too easily when it does.

And let's face it, it's usually going to be offering you a different path because it's unlikely to need to speak at all otherwise. Ultimately therefore it is most likely to be suggesting *change* and we humans generally aren't known for rushing towards that, not unless it's your shirt after a messy altercation with spaghetti Bolognese.

So the mind will invent reasons why *not* to listen and act; attempting to control by avoiding the unknown.

Returning to Olivia, as the official time for her appointment was drawing to a close, I was grateful that she confirmed the panic attack was over since my intuition had sensed it was very important that neither of us were focused on trying to hurry the attack to its conclusion. It certainly felt more appropriate to observe and witness it in the context that ultimately she knew she was safe, that it would pass and that she was very capable of handling the experience, rather than wishing it would be over as soon as possible. Accordingly I congratulated her on handling it so well and reminded her that as she now knows what her attacks feel like, she can permit her mind to be comforted by the fact that they are only temporary.

It's interesting to note that what might appear initially like a treatment going entirely pear-shaped, may actually (as in this case,) provide very positive advancements. So don't be put off when things seemingly aren't going according to plan.

A follow-up text to check that Olivia had been alright once she'd got home, delivered the response that she now felt much "lighter" and that she wanted to return for another treatment.

In fact further visits led to the following:

Third treatment six days later:

Feedback after the second visit – Feeling much better overall, though very tired. Had slept well for the last three nights which has been a very welcome change. Still feeling a little on edge. Very sensitive including her skin which has meant she has had to avoid wearing jewellery.

That day's observations - Olivia was able to lie down for the whole treatment and she felt she didn't need us to talk through it. Although she opened her eyes at times, she was mostly able to settle with her eyes closed. I worked without touch having taken note of her comments about her skin. During the treatment I got a very strong sense that her body had become overly sensitive because it is trying to get her attention – getting her to feel and go with her feelings rather than her thoughts. I shared this with Olivia afterwards. Also that as I held my hands over the area of her heart, I was given images of her heart being supported in a golden light which then changed into a little bird that really wanted to be allowed to sing.

I drew her attention to the previous conversation we had had that her heart wants to pursue gardening in some way, and that, although she must go with her own intuition and interpretation, I did get a feeling that the bird wanted to sing *"listen to your heart and your heart's desires"*. Olivia loved this image and when she came to put her coat on as she was leaving, we noticed how her scarf was covered in little bird images. We shared a knowing smile with each other.

Synchronicity – don't you just love it! The Universe has many beautiful ways of helping to get a message through.

Fourth treatment twelve days later:

Feedback after the third visit – Olivia had been feeling better. She had more energy and until recently, better sleep. She had been doing much more than usual because her mother was staying with her, and so she had been to London and Cambridge. She noted how in the past that would have made her very anxious, however actually she had coped very well. The last two days it felt as if her sleep has begun to deteriorate, so I said it was probably good timing for her to be here receiving another Reiki treatment.

That day's observations – Olivia felt the energy very strongly today, particularly whilst I was over her ankles. I shared how her energy felt to me like a moon shining on a summer's evening, a silent power.

Fifth treatment seventeen days later:

Feedback after fourth visit – Olivia felt well. She had been regaining the weight that she lost with all of her anxiety. She had lost ten kilograms, but now only needed to regain another four. Olivia was in great trepidation over a forthcoming hospital appointment in a couple of days and was hoping the Reiki would be able to calm her. The hospital would be carrying out a gastroscopy.

That day's observations – Towards the end of the treatment, when she would be more connected to her inner wisdom and less in her logical mind, I asked Olivia *"if the Reiki were able to calm you before and during this hospital procedure, what colour would it be?"* She replied that it was yellow and at the end of the session she told me she could see that the colour had been flowing up from her feet. I suggested that she link to the same yellow colour before and during her hospital appointment, using it to help her feel as calm as possible.

Sixth treatment six days later:

Feedback after fifth visit – Olivia felt both very well and that things had improved a lot. Having always been in her thoughts all the time she was now definitely finding some *"mind space"*. The hospital investigation had been okay. They had discovered that she had gastritis which needs treatment through diet and some medication. They expected her to have been experiencing pain from the condition but she confirmed it was only causing her discomfort. The medication was designed to heal the lining of her stomach, but they also established that she had a valve in her oesophagus which didn't close properly causing acid reflux, for which there is no orthodox cure. Olivia wanted to use the Reiki just as a top-up today as she told me she is now so much less in her mind.

That day's observations – The Reiki delivered a lot of energy into Olivia's stomach area today. Consequently she has decided to have a few more treatments in quick succession to see how much Reiki can help her in this direction.

Seventh treatment eight days later:

Feedback after sixth visit – Olivia said that she feels very well overall. She had suffered on the previous Tuesday because on *"feeling so well"*(!) she had had a lunch with her husband and it had included Teriyaki sauce which obviously did not agree with her. She had experienced a headache the day afterwards too.

Olivia knows that diet is going to play an important part in her health but it had been a sign of her feeling so good that she had risked the sauce in the first place. Since then she had compensated with eating a lot of vegetables and felt back on track. Olivia had felt so good anxiety-wise that she had just re-started acupuncture. She had been using this form of therapy before she came for Reiki as it had really helped her to relieve tension in her shoulders, but her anxiety attacks had put paid to continuing because she felt that she would worry too much to be able to lie down and accept needles. This week she had felt strong enough to go back, and it had helped her again.

Olivia had booked to go on a gardening course at a nearby college in the New Year (*fabulous*). She looked very happy at the thought of going there.

That day's observations – During the Reiki I asked Olivia to place her hand on her heart to ask for the colour most helpful to healing her stomach/acid reflux. The colour was yellow. She was able to see yellow flowing down inside her during the treatment. I had seen in my mind's eye during the session, a yellow waterfall cascading down from the top of her throat all the way to her abdomen. (*I noted that yellow was the colour she had given herself for calm regarding her hospital appointment last time. I get a sense that the anxiety and the health issues she is experiencing are all connected and that yellow has a vibration that will soothe her mind as well as her body. I spoke about this with her.)*

Eighth treatment seven days later: (*and last at time of writing*)

On asking how Olivia was, I got the response *"I am well."* (*How fantastic. What could be better than hearing that? I was so happy!*) Olivia told me that she had now halved her dose of anxiety medication and had had two days where she had taken nothing at all. (*In Olivia's first consultation she had shared that her GP had prescribed medication for her anxiety - tablets to be taken each day at her discretion.*) She felt that she had some anxiety worrying about whether she should have taken medication on the days that she chose not to, but actually she had been fine without it. (N.B. *All issues of medication levels should remain between a client and their GP so I simply acknowledged the information but didn't comment.*) Olivia is pursuing her gardening – working in a local charity garden for some experience before she starts her course next year. (*Well, I could comment about that – how wonderful. Her smile was telling me the joy that such a step was giving her.*) Olivia told me that she felt so much better than when she first came to me. (*How I love my job!*)

An additional consideration when you are working with highly anxious people, is to remember that it can be comforting for them to know where you are and what you are doing. So ask yourself if it is a good idea to disappear behind them to start a Reiki session at their head? My answer would be no. That doesn't prevent you from starting your treatment at the top of their body, but you may need to work a little differently to normal. If you typically start behind the head and go out of their line of vision as a consequence, then try standing to one side of them and placing your hands above or on their crown so that you can still retain eye contact. Alternatively you might begin at the feet/ankles so that your recipient can see exactly where you are and what you are doing.

Actually, let me more generally recommend experimenting with beginning treatments in different positions on or over the body. Having been led to believe it was correct to start at the head (even though the hand position for doing so had been unspecified), it was several years before I even thought to question this approach.

However, since letting my intuition take more of a lead, you will find me frequently beginning for example at the ankles, which subsequently I read other Practitioners favour when the recipient has been experiencing emotional issues.

Experiment. Go on, I'm sure a part of you wants to.

Over time you are likely to encounter a variety of professional scenarios, some of which will feel very challenging, so do be kind to and supportive of yourself. In all treatment scenarios, work within parameters that are comfortable (if a *little* testing) for *you* and that *you* feel equipped to deal with. Self-awareness is the key to how to approach them. Sense whether this is a challenge sent to enable you to grow your skills and expand your expertise (i.e. to continue whilst asking for as much intuitively-led guidance as can be made available to you), or whether it is asking you to realise that it is beyond your current level of ability or that another professional would be better equipped to handle the situation (i.e. refer your client on to another).

Ultimately your job is to provide Reiki energy. That is what Reiki therapists offer. And when you know how to allow the energy to flow through you, you can handle a Reiki treatment.

And take heart. When we are starting out I believe The Universe ensures that the vast majority of appointments will provide you simply with a perfect landscape in which to connect to this beautiful energy we call Reiki, whilst enabling your clients to feel the wonder and delight that only immersing themselves in their life force energy can bring.

Reiki Is Change

The practical considerations of handling more challenging treatments are one thing, but I can almost guarantee that becoming a Reiki Practitioner will raise some emotional ones too. Of course that's hardly surprising, since Reiki is a tool for self-awareness and development, and so naturally asks us to look at our relationship to the world around us.

Over the next few chapters, we'll consider some emotional challenges that you're likely to encounter in yourself, as well as some you'll see in your clients.

The important point to consider here, is that Reiki brings *change*.

Reiki will be asking you and your clients to make adjustments in life. All for the highest good, you understand, but the status quo won't do. Reiki doesn't want us to stay stuck in out-dated emotional and behavioural patterning, and will help highlight where we'd benefit from movement or alteration. Remember this particularly when working with others. Because as a Practitioner you are offering change, and that won't appeal to everybody.

After all, it can be rather dramatic. I have had people tell me, as they've got off the therapy couch, that they've now decided to get divorced, or leave their job. Big, life-changing acts.

And yet some people don't even want to heal their body, let alone their life situation. I know I found this startling when I first heard about it from David, my teacher.

Whilst on my Reiki Master course, he described a client who came to him ostensibly with the intention of healing a physical issue. However, he understood at the consultation stage, that she was receiving such a catalogue of benefits from having the condition that, surprisingly, she actually didn't want to heal at all.

She confirmed that she hadn't really wanted to attend the appointment, feeling others had pushed her into doing so. In fact she preferred to continue with some degree of inconvenience with her health, because it suited her to have her family treat her with additional compassion and kindness as a consequence.

This had obviously been a very frank conversation and the reasons clearly discussed. Sometimes however, it is not quite so obvious and for the Practitioner this can really be both a disappointment and a frustration, particularly where someone wants to heal but only so far…

A client of mine back in 2009, whom I shall refer to as Melanie, came to me suffering with a dis-ease called Sjögren's (pronounced 'Shore Gruns') Syndrome. I had never heard of the condition, and frankly was exceptionally grateful for this, both on my and anyone else's behalf, as the condition is a saddening list of symptoms that derive from the immune system attacking the body, especially its bodily secretions. A beautiful, and previously very active individual, now had constant pain and discomfort as her companion. Someone who had taken pleasure in life's more adventurous opportunities, such as sky diving and rugby, was finding it an accomplishment to swim once a week.

On her first visit, I noticed how the description of her symptoms included many references to war and battles.

White cells *'attacking'*, her body *'fighting itself'* etc. And so my first response was to invite Melanie to begin to change her relationship in this regard.

It seems a basic principle to me that when we want to support and work with our body (which must surely be the optimum foundation for healing it), then it is central to connect it to as much love as possible. Physically, of course, but also mentally. How we talk to it, and about it, is likely to play a part in its recovery.

The Reiki treatment felt very strong. Beautiful waves of light energy cascading through her body. And it felt very positive when Melanie booked to come back only a week later for another appointment.

That following session felt much more powerful, and it was as if her whole body opened up fully to receive the healing vibrations that I was helping her to connect to or, maybe more accurately, become aware of. So when she returned for a third treatment, you can imagine my absolute delight as Melanie excitedly told me that she had felt so much more energised in the last seven days that she had completed over ninety percent of her Thesis. She felt that otherwise she would have written a maximum of only one or two chapters. She now only had her conclusion to put together. Hoorah.

She shared with me how both her husband and her hairdresser had noticed a very positive difference in her. A big enough transformation that her hairdresser had thought she must have recently returned from a holiday. It felt like the most magnificent high. Exactly what had attracted me to being a Practitioner was being played out before me and in glorious technicolour, until…

The very next week revealed a key part of being therapist. It is unfortunately unlikely that a healing journey will involve only a steady climb towards better health. So wonderfully exciting is the sight of physical improvement in someone, that it can seem equally crushing when the reverse happens. And so it was with a very heavy heart that I listened as Melanie explained how she had had one of the worst weeks health-wise in a *long time*.

She had experienced bad pain, an inability to sleep, very sore joints, headaches. The last two days had seen some lessening of these, but all in all, the week had not been a good one. I felt myself deflate like a balloon which had once had the oh-so-happy task of taking part in a birthday celebration, but was now back to being the little piece of flat rubber in which it had begun its life.

This is where we have to stay strong and trust.

If we were discussing a case study from, say a weight-loss clinic, I guess we would not be too surprised if the story included a few episodes when things went in the wrong direction on several occasions. It would seem perfectly admissible that someone who was doing really well for a few weeks, suddenly had a bit of a downturn. They had a few celebratory events to go to and the chocolate cake was quite understandably requiring their attention. Or several less than happy situations had led to an emergency intake of ice-cream. Yes, we can all get that.

I think it is harder to allow setbacks in the healing trade, particularly if, as is likely in the early days of being a therapist, you tie in your value as a Practitioner too greatly with the results each of your clients shows you. But remember that you are not responsible for your client's responses. You are responsible for connecting them to Reiki energy, and frankly what they do with it is their business. And so we have to be satisfied with our knowledge that making that connection for them will be having a positive effect at some level, however visible or invisible the result.

And let's not forget the Herxheimer Reaction. *"Naturally, I consider it regularly Sarah"*. Well actually you might do without realising it, as it is more commonly referred to as a 'healing crisis' and whilst it may well have been covered on your training, if it hasn't, it is worth being aware of.

It is generally recognised that a 'healing crisis' or some might more comfortingly call it a 'healing reaction' (let's not panic here), can occur where a temporary worsening of symptoms is experienced as the body goes through the process of healing. This is relevant to all forms of therapy and not specifically to Reiki.

Usually only lasting a matter of hours or a couple of days as a maximum, it can be off-putting to someone new to complementary therapy, because they may assume that it is the therapy that is causing more issues than it is resolving.

It was this 'healing reaction' that Melanie and I agreed was explaining the downturn in her health.

Back with me a week later and Melanie was telling me that she had felt "buzzy" for the forty eight hours after her last treatment and had been sleeping better, feeling better, happier and less tired.

A week after that and she was saying how she was feeling "fantastic". Happily she was telling me how she was now coping really well. She was much calmer and the people that she works with were all noticing how much more relaxed and less tense she was.

I asked her to rate her health on a scale of 0 – 10 where ten would represent her health at its worst and it was so wonderful to hear her say that she felt she was at five. This was on her sixth appointment. Brilliant.

Melanie felt so good she decided to extend the time between her appointments meaning I next saw her three weeks later.

One of the most special things about being a Reiki Practitioner is that you get the opportunity to witness and celebrate in the happiness of others. Since we had last met, Melanie had been for a blood test to establish the level of her 'C-reactive protein'. She informed me that in a healthy individual this would typically measure around two. Over the last four years hers had been at seventeen, but this week it had been down to less than eleven and a half.

What a precious moment - to see pure joy in another person.

Oh what a fantastic job I now have. There was not one comparable moment I could think of whilst in any of my previous work environments. This was the fabulousness of Reiki.

Melanie requested another three week cycle until her next treatment, but when I saw her then, she said that it was only for the first two of those weeks that things had continued to be really good for her. Now she was thinking that she had left it too long between appointments because she had had something of a downturn at the end of last week.

This is where you need to be an observer for your clients because when I asked what she had been doing since we last met, it included making three hundred cupcakes, walking six miles whilst *"pulling a child"* (her words not mine) who was too tired to cycle, some late evenings where work required her to stay on, and looking after some friend's chickens whilst they were away on holiday.

As people heal it can often make them think they can do more than they are really ready for. Please take note that it is common for clients not to realise that they are putting increasingly greater strains on their body as they begin to feel better. This reduces in their mind the progress they are making.

So I didn't actually see this as a major set-back. For me, it was confirmation that Melanie now had enough energy to take on many more activities. She just needed to pace herself more. So you can imagine with perhaps just a two week interlude between appointments, or certainly with a period where she was being less physically hard on herself, there was more good news on its way?

I never saw her again.

Actually that isn't entirely true, which makes the story harder for me.

If I had never seen her again I may have reasoned that a major event in her life had taken place which meant that she was no longer able to focus on her health. What if she had been made redundant and so could no longer afford the treatments? What if her husband had been posted abroad and she was now living in Turkey? I mean, anything could have happened, right?

So there was an uncomfortable moment when I was working in a local shop (which I had been doing part-time to boost my income) and I looked up from the counter to see...Melanie. I could tell she felt awkward. She tried to explain why she hadn't been back to see me and I tried to let her know that she didn't need to explain anything, that I was just happy to see her.

I can only take from this that people have to heal at their own pace. Whilst it would be logical to think that someone would pursue something that was having such a positive impact on their lives, the very fact that some don't raises a recurring theme, that healing is change. Reiki is change. Some people only want to change so much. A person's identity can be defined by a health condition. It can get to a point where some people ask themselves, *"Who am I if I no longer have _____ (health issue) ?"*

A different client came to me for a couple of treatments to counter-balance a busy work life. On her second session she suggested she book treatments at least once a month, though possibly every two weeks if circumstances allowed, because she had felt great benefits in a range of different ways. Then on her third appointment she explained that it would be her last. Her partner had noticed that she was "changing" and she didn't feel comfortable with that. She didn't want her to come again and so she wasn't going to.

Essentially we just have to allow the client to go as far as they want to go. After all, that is all that will ever happen because, as we've already mentioned, people heal themselves. If we were party planners and were asked to put together an event for someone, we could select a wonderful array of festivities and yet the level of enjoyment is only ever set by the individuals attending.

We cannot take responsibility for anyone else.

And I feel it worth mentioning here that this includes our partners. Many of my fellow Practitioners have partners who have no inclination to venture down the Reiki road, mine included. And initially, I found it difficult to respect that.

What felt like such an important and life-affirming path opening up to me, meant I wanted my husband (my closest friend) to appreciate all its gifts too. It took me a while to realise that I shouldn't attempt to steer anyone else into something simply because it feels fundamental to my life.

A human trait is that we often feel more comfortable when others think the same as us and have the same interests. It helps to validate our way of being.

Wanting my husband to look at life the same way that I do was my weakness. And the fact that he didn't do so was his gift to my strength. Not only has this meant that I have had to find my own power and not be dependent on him to find it, it has also engendered a healthy respect and raised the value I place in the diversity of life and the ways in which it is lived. It might otherwise have been too easy for me to fall into a trap of feeling that those involved in Reiki are more spiritual. Taking a 'them' and 'us' stance. Instead I only have to look at my husband to see someone who is full of compassion and kindness and know for certain that this isn't true.

It has proved to me that none of us have the 'right way' of living, just 'one way' and that is a very helpful understanding for me to hold in general, but perhaps even more so when working with my clients.

It has also helped me remain more grounded. Thereby helping my spiritual path by ensuring balance and inclusion.

Of course we can help others with our newly found Reiki skills, but Reiki is actually a personal journey and we need to acknowledge this. If we put all our attention on what we can do for other people, we are missing the point. And focusing daily on *self*-healing, *self*-awareness and development (inner work) ensures that the assistance we give to others is the best that we can provide at any moment in our lives. It is an approach that will keep us humble and acting for the highest good for all concerned.

Regular self-Reiki enables us to reveal ever-deepening levels of self-love, allowing us to assist others more easily to do the same.

I believe the more we heal ourselves, the more we have the capacity to heal others. As we bring out more unconditional love for ourselves, not only will that be reflected into the collective unconscious, it will also impact those we interact with throughout the day, rather than only those we meet in our therapy rooms. It will spread naturally through a kind of osmosis rather than through a need to want to fashion others in the image of ourselves.

Feeling Good Enough

The stronger focus on self-awareness that Reiki gives us, brings more opportunities for us to look at the emotional landscape in which we work. One aspect of this relates to another facet of your fee, by which I am referring to how much *time* you will allocate to each client.

This touches (well actually it is more likely to bump you right up against) the areas of self-worth and self-acceptance. That thorny issue of what makes you feel you are good enough or have done enough.

One clear way in which I have been regularly tested on whether I felt I was good enough was over the length of client appointments. Watch this one. How much time do you extend an appointment by, in order to feel that you have done all you can? I have definitely improved in this department because in my early years as a Practitioner, it was almost a given for me to make an hour's appointment extend to seventy five minutes.

I found the weight of providing treatments on a professional basis, coupled with a lack of surety as to the degree to which each person had been helped, often unsettled my mind. It was always that unknown which opened the door to my self-doubt, and meant any chance of assuredness vacated the building. Unfortunately this would more than likely happen *during* the treatment, rather than after it was over.

It has been entirely possible for me to go from the immense joy of feeling strong energy sensations channelling through my body, seemingly confirming the efficacy of my Reiki connection, to wondering whether that was being replicated in my client. If I then ever let myself consider how different their experience *could* be from mine, I found I was able to talk myself into worrying about the quality of the service I was providing. Then to compensate for any possible lack, it often felt as if the only thing to do was to give additional healing time and that's how extra minutes were regularly added to my sessions.

If you also regularly feel you need to over-run because you tell yourself you need to do more, then eventually like me, you will have to face the fact that this is not an objective assessment of a treatment, but a feeling of emotional inadequacy on your part.

Traditionally, appointments are scheduled to run for sixty or ninety minutes. And be assured this really does provide sufficient time for a complete treatment. (I'd prove this to myself with the responses I could receive when offering twenty minute taster treatments at school fund-raising pamper nights and the like, but obviously not so completely that I could believe such would be true for my *next* client.)

Within your chosen time-frame you need to allow for a consultation period at the start, the Reiki itself, coming-round time, post-treatment discussion, dressing (shoes and coat), payment and hopefully booking a future session (that would be nice wouldn't it?).

There's also a need for flexibility, because particularly the consultation and post-treatment discussion stages can be rather unknown quantities, varying greatly from person to person and appointment to appointment. Consequently it is impossible to gauge exactly how long you will need to allocate to each.

Extended pre-treatment consultations can make you feel that clients have in some way been short-changed regarding the Reiki, which can add another pressure to extend the treatment time to make up for it.

It is therefore well-worth realising the value of appointments in providing clients with an opportunity in which they can express themselves and, of equal importance, be listened to. This too is healing.

To overcome this issue, it might help you to actively intend for the Reiki to flow from the moment they have signed their agreement for their initial treatment, and at the time of greeting them on any future appointments. This way you can remind yourself that you are providing a Reiki-filled appointment however long they are actually lying on the couch.

Nowadays *I know* the Reiki energy is holding us both from the outset anyway. But in those earlier days I do believe the importance was in specifically intending it to be so. It's a little like when you learn to drive. At the beginning you need to consciously work through the procedure of how to make a gear change in order for it to happen. However, after a while, it is embedded in such a way that it becomes an unconscious reflex action as and when appropriate.

Since the consultation begins the appointment, at least there will always be sufficient time to accommodate those clients who require an extended period to express themselves. So the difficulty comes in deciding when to bring the Reiki to a close. (Actually though, I would argue that an appointment really begins from the first text, phone call or email that a prospective client initiates.)

With its likelihood of transporting the recipient into a deep, less consciously aware space, you will have to allow your client time to come back from that place and regain their full awareness before they are ready to safely get down from a therapy couch. It is a process which, in my opinion, should not be hurried.

Some people will open their eyes quickly. Others will be completely out of it. So much so, that if you've someone else arriving in the next few minutes, you'll be stressing to find balance. How do you allow your earlier client sufficient time to gently come back to full consciousness, whilst ensuring your therapy couch is unoccupied in time for the next person's arrival? The issue is often more acute on a first appointment – which type of client have you got, how long should you allow?

To a certain extent this may well depend on how tight to time you *need* to be. I never have an issue with giving a client additional time as long as this has nothing to do with my feeling inadequate, nor any abuse of my time by the client.

A fellow Practitioner (who would term herself as a spiritual healer and who incorporates other elements such as the use of Oracle cards and flower essences), told me once over a coffee, how annoying she was finding it to have clients that were becoming more and more demanding of her time. She was happy to run an hour's appointment for ninety minutes, but she was having clients who regularly demanded two hours and was exasperated by a woman who had been in her home for two and a half hours a few days before.

She was beginning to resent her flexibility in this matter. In truth it was getting totally out of hand.

Anyone at the point of feeling resentment, must come to terms with realising that they are out of balance. Such an emotion indicates that things have gone too far and adjustments need to be made.

The interesting question is, why?

She had been a therapist a great deal longer than myself. Why then was she suddenly having a run of clients who had so little regard for her time? The common factor in each instance was of course herself, so that was where the answer would lie. As we chatted we established that her appointment extensions grew out of a need to be needed. There was a certain satisfaction that she gained from being needed (more).

When we fail to recognise that our balance is being compromised, The Universe is incredibly clever at showing us. Larger and larger erosions of my friend's time were being accepted by her. Ultimately the situation had to be made so apparent there could be no denying there was an issue to be resolved.

It's no good blaming the client(s). We, by way of our energy, are the ones attracting them and it is up to us to set the terms and conditions in which we are prepared to work. We have to take responsibility and clearly define our boundaries. If clients are pushing us to significantly overrun, such as when the discussion of a mental image they've received during the treatment precipitates an in-depth recounting of a whole series of events in their life, then it is perfectly acceptable to mention (gently) that you have to clear the room for another appointment. I have only ever had a very apologetic response on such occasions – it has never caused a problem.

Other kind ways of signalling the conclusion of a session can be to fold away the blanket. Remove towels from the therapy bed. Turn up the lights (if you had dimmed them). Switch off any music. Pick up their coat.

I've not been immune from self-generated time issues though, which I shall hold my hand up to now.

Generally I've lived with a policy of having a half hour buffer between client appointments. This allows time for some over-run if *needed*. It also allows for practical tasks, such as changing towels and getting fresh water, writing up notes about the client who has just left and reading any notes about the client who is about to arrive. Great. There appears to be an acceptance by The Universe that this is perfectly reasonable and is therefore a structure I continue to employ.

Interestingly though, I noticed that if ever my focus changed from these worthy intentions and I began to *depend* on the half hour to assuage any thoughts of inadequacy on my part (by extending appointments to 'give more'), events would then conspire against me to highlight what I was doing.

Examples of this might be where I would have a client booking at 2:00pm and instead of the next client being able to come at 3:30pm they would tell me that it could only be 3:15pm because they must pick up their children from an after school club. Or I'd have two friends who would specifically ask me for my 10:00am and 11:00am sessions, so they could go on for lunch together afterwards.

Situations that compelled me to review working to time and which would enable the message to get through.

The other side of the coin is that when a client absolutely *needs* longer than the proposed hour, it seems to happen without causing any stress to my timetable. For instance three weeks before writing this I had a new client contact me, requesting an appointment on Saturday afternoon at 2:00pm. I already had another client booked for 12:00pm and just accepted that sometimes we have to be flexible and there will be more than the ideal gap between appointments.

This particular Saturday was also the first day of a holiday trip to Devon. My husband and I had arranged to travel by car late Saturday afternoon in the hope of missing most of the heavy traffic, yet still arriving at a reasonable time. The 2 o'clock start time would still fit in with our plans.

That Friday evening, however, I received a text from this second client (let's call her Samantha) saying that she had been in hospital all day and that she wasn't sure if she would be up to coming to her session tomorrow or not. Understanding her dilemma I wrote back to her that I would be at The Centre anyway and she could let me know how she felt on the day as long as it was by 1:00pm.

When she later confirmed she would like to come she kindly asked if it would suit me better to start her appointment an hour earlier, so that I wouldn't be left waiting for her to arrive. We agreed to meet at 1.15pm to allow for a changeover and then all was in place for a smooth transition. Excellent.

On the Saturday in question, my first client's appointment was very straightforward and she was on her way by about

1:02pm so all sorted for Samantha who had arrived nicely to time.

Samantha was a lovely woman whom I immediately warmed to. She was engaging and humorous. And quite frankly she needed a sense of humour, because there was a nigh-on exhaustive list of health issues and incidents that would have seen me as a jabbering wreck rocking in the corner of a room, should it have been a description of my life.

There was no request for even a modicum of pity in the forty minutes it took to summarise most of what had been going on for her, even though I knew I was getting the edited, abridged version. And don't forget, she had nearly cancelled because she had been in hospital most of the day before. This was due to an extremely debilitating headache/migraine which had been going on for the whole week. It had not been responding to the usually prescribed drugs and the symptoms had been worsening, including loss of vision. The hospital had been carrying out a myriad of neurological tests but it was thought that the onset of her condition had been stress-induced, which would be no surprise to anyone hearing her recent life résumé.

Her circumstances clarified, I then needed to explain a little about Reiki and how we would progress. It was leaving little time for the treatment but then of course she had been scheduled initially to finish at 3:00pm. Was she under any pressure to leave exactly at 2:00pm? With the answer in the negative I knew we could therefore just allow the energy to take its course. But I had little idea that it was going to be such an intense and emotional experience, and frankly was thinking that we'd still likely finish by 2:20pm.

The Reiki energy felt extremely powerful to me right from the very start. That doesn't always relate to how the client will experience it, but I knew a lot was happening whatever Samantha's perspective.

And then Samantha began to show signs of emotional upheaval. The Reiki was having a most definite impact and to the extent that I needed to check that she was alright to continue.

Now I'm sure that mind's eye images will have been covered as part of your training because they are such a key part of many people's experience within Reiki. Whether they are provided by the unconscious mind or the Soul/Inner Being, and how much these are one and the same thing, I can't be sure. But they are intrinsic to many people's Reiki journey. Some will see whole scenes play out before them, some just snapshot images and others will re-visit earlier life experiences. They may offer insights that assist in the healing, or they may be more enigmatic and remain coded as a language beyond our comprehension. Either way, they are often a part of the process.

Where pictures do form part of a recipient's experience, I feel it is most important for a client to evaluate for themselves why that image has come to them and what it could mean. That's not to say that I can't have my own interpretation which might legitimately be different to theirs, but I'd make clear that their understanding takes precedence. It's their image, sent to them for their healing.

Even when sharing images that have come to me as the Practitioner, I would still choose to hear the client's analysis in the first instance because it is always important to empower the client as much as possible. I don't want the possibility of their deference to my position of experience to in anyway lessen the value of their own answer. Maybe the picture had to come via me because they weren't at the correct level of consciousness to receive it, rather than that I would be best placed to understand it? Either way, it's good to ensure that they have the opportunity to decipher any meaning before putting forward my own, no matter how definite I feel.

After all, only they can know what an image, or phrase truly means to them. There can be no dictionary of terms because the language of each individuals' unconscious mind is like a tapestry, threads which when brought together create unique pictures, words or feelings shaped from events throughout their life, whilst we as outsiders might only be able to see the colour of the yarn.

It can be very helpful, however, to present *additional* viewpoints or *possible* understandings. Not least because you may receive really strong intuitive translations that have come to you on behalf of the client to ensure that they are delivered and not ignored.

We all mess up though, and just a couple of days ago I was too keen to express my opinion and it came out of my mouth before I knew it. The image in question had been one of a scarred heart with the Reiki energy gently softening those scars. With speech engaged well in advance of brain, I leapt forward with my explanation. When the client told me that she had felt it was the scars from the death of several of her children through miscarriages, I absolutely knew that that was her truth and it should have been the primary focus. It wasn't so much that there was a right and wrong, just that it should have been more to do with her feelings rather than mine.

Accordingly even when intuition tells me my message is highly valid, I would still choose to express it as a *possible* understanding which hopefully also avoids me putting 'my stuff' onto someone else through projection. This is where we project our own issues onto other people rather than facing them ourselves.

The good news is that we never need to interpret for someone else as we can simply share an image and leave it at that. As we develop our self-awareness together with our intuition we can then ensure we provide potential insight to our client's advantage.

Of course images don't always come. In fact a friend who completed her Reiki Master course with me used to regularly get images at every treatment she ran…until she didn't. One day they just seemed to be switched off. It became frustrating to her that months later they still hadn't returned and she had no way of knowing if they ever would.

Be aware too that images are not available to everyone – aphantasia describes the condition where a person has an inability to visualise mental images and it is thought to affect as many as one in fifty people.

Returning to the treatment with Samantha, what was significant on this occasion was that my intuition was telling me of the benefit of *inducing* an image to help her to work through the emotions that were bubbling up inside her. I asked her what her issues would look like if they were a shape, colour or object; she said they were like a large boil. I asked her what needed to happen to the boil.

She felt that it needed to burst and that the issue was right at the base of the boil. I suggested she allow herself to follow through on any action she felt guided to take (the answers had to come from her). A few moments later I asked her what was happening and she said that the imagery had changed. She was now looking at a volcano. Tears began to cascade down her face, followed by full-blown crying.

It's worth highlighting that even though I was at this time more than ten years into my Reiki Practitioner experience, such circumstances still remind me of the vulnerability of a client in any Practitioner's hands.

The more humbly and less egotistically I approach my work, the more help seems to be on offer.

I asked for the Reiki and my and Samantha's Souls/Inner Beings to guide us through the process, keeping thoughts on my energy being strong and supportive, yet compassionate and loving. Assistance from less physical levels is fortunately always on hand and I could somehow feel that we were being guided. We didn't have to know how this was going to work out, rather just trust that we had come together so that whatever was needed to happen, would happen.

A quick glance up at the clock revealed it was 2:35pm. Thank goodness time could be of no consequence because the intensity of her experience could not have been interrupted with a need to vacate the room for another appointment (so a big thank you to The Universe for arranging this).

However here I was feeling the possibility of having initiated a situation (by asking her to visualise the energy) which was beyond my skills to handle. I never want put a client in a position that pushes them further than we are both able to deal with. This can be a difficult call because how can I know what the safe parameters are? The barometer for me is whether I have been mentally pushing for advancements, or whether they have come naturally and my ego feels out of the equation. Fortunately the push had very much felt as if it had come from somewhere other than myself. Whilst there was some disquiet in my mind, being unsure if I was out of my depth, somehow asking myself that very question meant that I felt I wasn't, and was therefore working from a place of trust rather than control.

Samantha was now becoming very agitated and then told me she was scared. All I could think to do was to give her control reminding her she could stop at any time. But she wanted to continue.

As part of the consultation, Samantha had mentioned that she was a Christian and so it felt right to tell her to call on God and or angels to assist her and keep her safe, whilst I increased my sense of holding her in love.

When I asked her what was happening now, she said that the volcano was empty and my thoughts immediately acknowledged the similarity between a 'boil' and a 'volcano' and their need to erupt. The fact that the volcano was empty made me believe that the process of eruption had occurred during her tearful outburst and that that had been the process of letting go.

Asking her what she was then experiencing, she told me that the land was very barren. And then a different type of crying began as she went on to say that she could now see a lone tree beginning to grow out of this waste land. A smile broke through the tears, the tree symbolised *"hope."*

This was powerful. The energy was immense and goose bumps ran down my arms signalling its potency.

From then on the session reduced in intensity. I made sure to confirm that she was *safe* and reminded her she had a very definite sign of hope – encouraging her to fully connect with and focus on only the new and positive expression of her energy.

Bringing the session to a close, we discussed what had taken place and I gave her the opportunity to share anything else which had happened. She then told me how it had felt as if her arms were being weighted or held down (typical Reiki sensation), how her head and neck had at times felt like it was being pulled, and how she had felt a lot of heat, in various places, from the moment we had started.

We both knew that something transformational had taken place.

As she began to put her shoes back on the clock read 3:15pm. But I knew The Universe was happy with the time extension, and I would be leaving for home and my holiday not much later than I was expecting if we'd been starting at the original appointment time of 2:00pm.

Whilst this was an unusual scenario, it does show the advantage of asking upfront if an appointment time needs to be strictly observed.

Ultimately the Practitioner must accept responsibility for being the official timekeeper. As someone who is probably a giver by nature, and therefore more prone to extending an appointment than not, think of the client who has booked with a view to finishing at the perfect time to catch a train, or pick up their partner. Extending an appointment is *not* always a good thing. It also shows a lack of trust that the energy can do whatever it needs to do without being bound by the positioning of hands on a clock face. Time to trust!

Establishing a client's schedule will enable you to evaluate approximately when to begin bringing them round. If they surprise you by taking less time than average, you can use the spare minutes to discuss *more fully* any observations, images, sensations etc. that the Reiki generated.

I find it good practice to finish a treatment by softly whispering something along the following lines, whilst gently laying a hand on one of their shoulders:

"And now it's time to bring all your energy and awareness back into the here and now. Have a stretch of fingers and toes, and when you feel ready open your eyes and see how good you feel."

As stated earlier, my recommendation is to let people *know* when the treatment is over and they can open their eyes, whilst leaving them to choose the exact moment – ensuring they feel ready to do so. Beginning with the word 'and', softens the sentence. Suggesting they 'see how good they feel' places their focus towards the positive. If they have difficulties coming round, then very gently saying their name usually does the trick.

Now I did say that if your client gets up more quickly after the treatment than you had bargained for, that you can then allow *additional* time to *"discuss more fully"* any observations etc. Because I do believe that a key part of any appointment includes the ability for individuals to express and discuss their experiences of Reiki with you.

Never under-estimate how healing it can be for them to voice what was going on for them during their treatment. Not least because this validates that what they felt was both 'usual' (within the confines of Reiki) and also encourages them to explore their relationship to any images, phrases or sensations that the treatment generated. Otherwise it is all too easy for their logical mind to discount valuable inner messages.

Ensuring there is a period to reflect and share feedback can really help a client own their healing, and open the doorway that accesses a more spiritual way of viewing life. *Their* body, *their* mind, *their* connection to their life-force energy has provided interactions beyond logic and everyday physical experience.

Accordingly Reiki can often be the tipping point for people to notice synchronistic messages or maybe to at least value them more highly.

One woman who came to me for her first ever session found it included a great deal of mental imagery. She was fascinated that her mind could even produce such information. When we began to discuss what it could mean, her excitement grew and there was a definite realisation that we were witness to a little magic taking place between her and a more esoteric part of her being.

Although she never returned, there had been a huge reward in a text message she sent me later that afternoon. Having gone into town to do some shopping she had passed by a shop that, as part of a yearly held promotion for local artists, had unexpectedly had a painting in its window. It was of a wolf – exactly like one of the images she had been shown during the Reiki. This had led her to enter the shop (she'd never been in it before) and feel drawn to a book containing a message that I sensed would be the start of a life-long journey exploring her spiritual self. How beautiful.

Having mentioned extending treatments, it's worth noting that very infrequently but nevertheless now and again, there can be a treatment where perhaps ten minutes before the end time, I just get a huge intuitive sense of, *'that's enough'*. In such circumstances I adjust my intention to simply holding the recipient in a loving state, noting the healing is complete.

Another way I feel I've been asking myself to feel good enough during my Reiki journey, has been over-judging myself in relation to other Reiki Practitioners. More explicitly, to stop doing it!

I am a little ashamed to say I began my Reiki journey with a great deal more competitive attitude than it is comfortable for me to own up to. Accordingly I was envious when others appeared to be doing better than I was, and additionally it meant that a part of me felt that I was vying with others for clients.

There was a struggle between my heart and my emotions on this subject for a long time. My heart, and even my reasoned mind, would agree with the statement that we will receive the clients that we are meant to receive. That our energetic vibration attracts those that we are supposed to encounter for the learning and ultimate highest good of both parties. And yet my emotions were stuck in a childhood pattern of feeling *"there won't be enough for me"*.

When my emotions eventually caught up with my inner knowing, and I could *feel* the truth behind the understanding, there were opportunities to confirm just how right my heart had been.

I remember a very liberating and heart-felt sensation when every part of me finally came into alignment with what I had been telling myself and others for so long.

A potential client had phoned me to arrange an appointment and their extremely busy schedule had led me to believe that I just wasn't going to be able to accommodate them. We had seemingly exhausted the possibilities of our diaries ever matching that week. In times past I would have felt greatly stressed by this and it would have led me to push to make the appointment later in the month. However this didn't come as an option as the conversation had begun with a clear directive that a treatment was needed within the upcoming seven days.

And then I just heard myself saying very clearly that *"there is another therapist that offers Reiki whom I could put you in touch with"* and I really meant just that. For once there was no *hidden* annoyance or frustration from failing to find a mutually convenient appointment time – where you say the 'right' thing in the 'right' way but you know deep down you don't quite mean it. This was definitely expressing my ability to feel that I was in no way losing work and how some people are meant to come to you whilst others not, but that you shouldn't feel abandoned or let down when things seemingly don't go your way.

The energy change in the midst of the phone call was palpable. It suddenly switched within the merest split second of my realising the situation was not affecting my self-esteem. At this point the woman concerned told me *"no, it has to be you, you were highly recommended, I'm sure I can make it on Friday so let's go with that"*. How ironic. The very moment I am utterly convinced that this has nothing to do with my self-worth, it receives a huge boost by hearing that I'm highly recommended.

Now as much as I believe we should avoid allowing our self-esteem to be dependent upon what others think of us, I do believe that how we value ourselves has a direct effect on our life experiences. Let me share some numbers with you.

22

16

12

14

4

13

19

19

24

26

26

19

These are from the year 2014 and they list the number of client appointments I had in consecutive months. See that number four in bold? Well that's a month that I suffered a complete lack of self-belief. For some crazy unconscious reason, I lost my confidence and spent the best part of four weeks worrying that my abilities with Reiki weren't good enough. I couldn't seem to help it. The more I told myself to stop, to realise my years of experience meant something, to review case studies where the results appeared very favourable, my mind continued to pick at a wound I thought was a thing of the past. Any distraction which would momentarily allow a scab to form merely drew my attention back to pick at it again, putting its healing further out of reach.

It wasn't until I entered my client booking figures in a spreadsheet and saw how perfectly respectable they'd been in the months beforehand, that it shook me out of what had been a very unwelcome spiral of negative thoughts and somehow put me back on track.

The thoughts had appeared to come unbidden. I've no idea what started the pattern, but it did prove to me that whilst I cannot control events in my life, my emotional response undoubtedly has an impact on them.

Even with my now healthier level of self-belief, there will be months with fewer clients than I would wish for. If you speak to other self-employed people, from a range of differing professions, they will often have similar issues. Some months lots of work; others much less. I don't know what makes the difference. However, I recognise that it can be for reasons that I cannot see in advance but that I welcome nearer the time. Frequently when I am bemoaning what looks like a lack of appointments in the week ahead, as it approaches I receive an invitation from a friend or an offer of a trip away which immediately turns dissatisfaction and frustration into gratitude. It happens also when I'd benefit from a push to complete an outstanding task which I could otherwise claim to be too busy to complete. Sometimes such occasions will coincide with tiredness or the onset of a cold and I can thank The Universe for orchestrating time off at exactly the right moment.

Note to self, quieter weeks are not always bad news.

Being a therapist often means going with the ebb and flow; just realise that your energy will play a part but don't beat yourself up when things seem less than at their best. Avoid letting your mind talk you into a permanent slump and notice whether, as in my case, energy changes are often far more about your relationship with yourself than with other people.

Also remember that there are many elements to the number of appointments your business can generate, and some will be out of your control. For instance, if you live in a remote part of the country, it is very unlikely you will generate as many clients as living in a town or city.

(By the way, the average number of appointments per month for me currently stands around seventeen, though I'm not encouraging you to compare yourself to anyone else, because you know you can never rate your worth by numbers don't you!)

The Importance Of Letting Go

Another aspect of your journey into self-awareness is likely to focus on your relationship between control and letting go.

What's more, aspects of this will likely feature very early on; firstly because letting go is implicit in learning to work with something that you connect to, or become aware of, but don't really '*do*'; secondly because another aspect of letting go is the release of any attempt or wish to control the outcome of a treatment.

In the keenness of wishing for the best end result that a client could possibly want, and therefore what they would *consciously* have requested – *"my back hurts, fix it"* – I know when I first trained, I had a strong tendency to wish for exactly that.

There was the knowledge that Reiki goes where it needs to go, doing what it needs to do, but also a slight anxiety that I might not be (doing) enough to allow it to do so. I wanted to *direct* the energy. I wanted the feedback that the main issue (as it appeared to the client,) was healing in some way. And yet I could also recognise that it would always be beyond my limited thinking, that I could decide on the route by which that was possible.

I could relate to the fact that in order for their knee to recover, an individual's starting point might actually be to love themselves more – love themselves enough to feel that they deserved to heal for instance. So that the pre-cursor to mobility in that joint would actually be an emotional change, something far removed from the client's desired outcome, and something neither of us might be aware of.

Yes the wisdom behind Reiki was indeed where my trust should lie. But you have to let go in order to be in that state of trust, and that was something I needed to learn.

That was not just in relation to my job. I sense that releasing control and trusting in the wisdom and direction of The Universe/Soul/Inner Being (call it what you will) is a key foundation for moving towards a balanced life in general. It's just that when you live at the sharp end when working as a Reiki Practitioner, the value of letting go and trusting is heightened accordingly.

It is in the relinquishing of attempts to control every aspect of our lives that we enable ourselves to build our trust in it. The same can be said for Reiki.

Such a methodology goes hand in hand with working from the heart rather than the head. To me the head, or mind (through which we try to exert control), is in some way linked to my understanding of the ego. The mind/ego is brilliant when used correctly – try planning to catch a train without it – but what is so clearly an asset in certain circumstances, becomes an overhead as soon as it becomes over-used.

I have just slowed down over the word *overhead*. It is a message in itself. I have in the past just used this as a term that an accountant might use to express something to pay out for, as opposed to income coming in. Now I revisit the word with a different emphasis. It is saying in this context "over…head" as in too much in your head, as in exactly what I am talking about!

Have you ever re-read a self-help book and found that you experience it in a completely different way from the earlier read? Perhaps something the first time around didn't have any resonance with you or make any sense, only a few years later you find it is speaking as if it were your very own words on the page.

We can only see the world from our own perspective. When we are open enough to change that perspective, completely new insight can come up and hit us in the face with the full force of the staggeringly obvious. Whereas it might have been so hidden before, that it could have been written in red ink, seventy two font size, on an A3 piece of card and we still would not have been able to see what was written.

We cannot know (mind-read) what a client is really wishing for or wanting. Perhaps more importantly we cannot know what is right for them. Faith in the innate intelligence of Reiki is therefore critical.

Reiki asks us to feel that faith, not only in our role as Practitioner, but also in our lives in general.

Have you have ever experienced for yourself, or seen in another, a situation arise which seems only bleak or negative at the time, but as (your or the other person's) life unfolds further, you realise the importance of that event having taken place? It evidently required hindsight to give it reason, meaning or benefit.

Sometimes we are asked to trust that the essence of life is holding us and supporting us, through challenges which ultimately have been constructed to move us forward. It is seemingly an all too frequent aspect of human nature that we tend to change direction only when pressurised to do so;

that whilst we can comfort ourselves in day-to-day familiarity, however restrictive and uninspiring that is, we simply continue repeating our way of being. Consequently we will often be forced into making alterations only as a result of increasing stress.

Thus, what initially appears pure adversity, can in fact precipitate our most constructive turning points, such that we can acknowledge that we would not have blossomed in the way that we have, had we not been met with those challenges.

A controlling mind would attempt to eradicate such life-changing events.

It's not uncommon for me to see people who ostensibly have come to heal a particular physical condition, yet I sense they are somehow being led to the *experience* of Reiki as much, or possibly more than the healing.

Take my own situation. The issue with my fingers led me into the world which I now so gratefully inhabit. It began my spiritual journey. It was the catalyst that opened my awareness to things beyond the physical.

It puts me in mind of a client who was visiting from Russia, who had a couple of appointments with me, during his stay. Whilst his main focus concerned a digestive issue, it was the magical non-physical aspects of the treatment that captured his attention. He kindly gave me the following feedback:

"Thanks so much for the wonderful treatments the past days. You have truly opened up a new world to me that I only dreamed existed, but never before had tangible proof

of. You have changed my life forever by giving me that knowledge."

How wonderful Reiki can be in this respect. As Practitioners we are able to offer far-reaching effects from one relatively small amount of time in someone's company.

In this vein we often cannot be sure what the best outcome for a client would be – whether the part we play in their healing journey is as clear cut as they might consciously desire – through the alleviation or removal of symptoms that have been manifesting in their body. Or whether the best outcome is to introduce them to a world beyond the usual norms of human existence – to make them aware of their Soul connection.

Naturally I'm sure we would opt for a mixture of both, but our job of providing access to the energy we term Reiki is rather like giving money to a child at Christmas. If it is a true gift, then you can't add strings to its giving. You are not in a position to dictate in which way the money should be spent. You must give it with your heart in the simplest hope (and trust) that in *some way*, it will make a positive difference to the recipient. Whether or not *their* idea of a positive difference is something you would approve of.

I now see Reiki in those terms. We might wish for one thing rather than another for our clients, particularly when there is such mutual joy in a health condition healing, but as long as we give our connection to the energy in good faith, our job is done.

That has been my over-riding feeling when giving Reiki to someone with a terminal prognosis. If a recipient uses it to feel they can more easily let go of life, then the gift is still a good one.

I have had only very limited experience of working with people in such circumstances. The first was many years ago when a son had contacted me regarding his father. The man was bed-ridden in the latter stages of cancer, and consequently required home-based treatments. The Reiki was being sought as a way to bring comfort and ease where possible. However, no one involved had ever had Reiki before, and so it felt like a huge privilege to have my services requested at such a delicate time.

[Please note that legally it is an offence to offer treatment, prescribe a remedy or give advice for cancer, if you work in the UK. Of course you may still give Reiki to someone with the condition, but you must ensure that you neither verbally, nor in writing via any marketing documentation, claim to treat cancer in any way.]

The son and daughter-in-law asked whether they could remain in the room for the duration of the treatment, to which I happily agreed. As it happened they were both able to sense energy changes in themselves, which back then I found particularly gratifying. More recently I have come to expect that experience and, as already mentioned, instruct those who are accompanying children or vulnerable adults that they may benefit from the energies too. Back then it was new territory, as I had never given a treatment where anyone else but the client was present.

Thankfully, and more importantly, the father also felt very positive benefits. We continued with treatments for a couple of months. There was no expectation of recovery and when no further appointments were made, I knew why. This was confirmed when I came across the son, about a year or so later, in my local town centre. It touched me greatly to hear that the Reiki had brought all of them some much needed relief and comfort, during such difficult and dark times. The son was able to tell me that it had made his father's passing a little easier.

Assisting the transition of someone who is ready to leave this life is one thing. However, I'm sure we can all acknowledge how much more emotionally stressful it is for a Practitioner to encounter someone in similar circumstances who is showing a great desire to continue to live. In such instances we must comfort ourselves with the understanding that on some other level, beyond our own limited comprehension, there will be good reason to die. It is not (always) ours to know. It strikes me that the transformation we generally speak of as the tragedy of death may be a perspective only held on this side of the veil.

What I fundamentally do believe, however, is the advantage of holding in your heart the absolute acknowledgement that anything is possible, whilst giving Reiki. In that way you will ensure you never restrict what can be achieved via the energy connection you provide. For me it is also a way of remaining more neutral to the outcome, because there is less self-assessment of what you are doing as you are doing it.

It is vital to raise with any client, whatever their condition, that we can never know where a Reiki treatment will take them – but then that is true for any therapy.

We may never be given the opportunity to recognise even when significant changes are taking place, as they may exist only outside our conscious awareness. Then again, it may be that they are so obvious that everyone involved can celebrate. To be a Reiki Practitioner you need to find your comfort in either scenario.

And as I stated earlier, you may well be called upon to highlight your client's advancements on their behalf. Look again at Melanie's situation. It was not until she recounted to me the sheer volume of activity she was engaging in, that she could appreciate the possibility of feeling so tired, without it signifying a backward step in her health.

As well as instances where an increase in activity has led to a lack of appreciation of improvements, there will be other times when a client ignores the progress they're making. Most often this occurs when they have a general trait of feeling that they are not good enough, consequently, that they have never done enough – one belief being a reflection of the other. This results in a client constantly looking at the other parts of their lives or body that are still not functioning well, rather than spending (at least a little) time acknowledging the improvement they have made.

They begin focusing only on what still needs addressing, to the point where they can have forgotten their progress. Keep your eyes and ears open for this because it is where your third party observations can really empower your client. You can remind them that they came to you to achieve something and that they have achieved it! Help them to stop their minds from running on to catalogue the next thing on their list.

I often ask my clients to sit for a moment and inwardly congratulate themselves on what a difference they are making to their lives, particularly regarding emotional advancements that are easy to miss.

It may be that the very fact they haven't said anything about a situation that had previously been greatly troubling them that indicates it would be helpful to ask them about it.

For many it can come almost as a magnificent surprise that it is no longer a cause for concern. *"Oh, yes, now you ask, I met with her last Tuesday and everything was fine. I couldn't believe how well it went. I just seemed to express my feelings without all of the anger I would usually have felt. And she accepted what I said and so it's all okay."*

"Okay? Okay? This is huge for you. This is amazing. You had been stressing about this for ages, to the point that you hadn't been sleeping..."

You get my drift.

Too many people just continue on looking for what else doesn't appear to be working well for them.

Make them see their successes. Be on the look-out as much for what doesn't get said, as what does.

Surprisingly it can happen over health issues too. There are times when it is only by questioning how their stomach has been feeling over the last three weeks, that we can celebrate the fact that it's so much better, and the very reason why we are only talking now about their left arm.

People can find it hard to let go of the need to find fault in themselves. So shine a light on their achievements. Where they have successfully released an issue, make them take the time to savour the results.

Where it doesn't appear that there is much cause to cheer after a few treatments, it might be that Reiki is just not the right treatment for them. In my heart of hearts I always feel there has been some benefit, even if the result is too hidden to openly acknowledge. At that point though, think about suggesting they try another type of therapy or therapist. There are going to be times when we are not the right person to work with a certain individual.

For instance, I remember treating someone who had come to see me because I had replaced the Practitioner who was on maternity leave. The client in question made it very obvious that I didn't make the grade. I think the reason came down to the fact that I didn't provide her with the level of 'psychic' feedback my predecessor had seemingly always done. Whilst she did note she could feel many of the physical sensations that she had felt with her previous therapist, it was clearly, in her opinion, a sub-standard treatment that I had given her. (It is worth noting that I experience a wide range of variations in the amount of messages I receive during Reiki sessions. At times there is simply an energy exchange and nothing more. At others possibly a whole catalogue of feedback is given to me to share with the client. I might get anything from symbolic images, to phrases, song lyrics, or a sense of the emotional tone of my client's situation. I have to accept what needs to be shown is shown to me, and be content when it appears there is nothing to add.)

On another occasion, a different person but similar circumstance, led me to be directly compared to that same other therapist. Whilst very glad of the honesty involved, I was a little crushed by the fact that the client said she hadn't really felt anything at my hands in comparison.

If this happens to you, don't take it personally. I guess that might be easier said than done if you are early on in your career. I was fortunate to be experienced enough by this point to largely be unconcerned, though not completely unaffected.

Ultimately a client relationship is much like meeting new people in any environment – there will be those that love you from the very start, and those that just never click with you. (I'm sure it will be their loss!)

Maybe in that latter circumstance (because Reiki is such a great teacher), it could simply be a way of asking you to value yourself whatever response you get from others. Consider if the whole scenario was expressly devised as a beautiful way for you to establish your own sense of worth, without being dependent on validation from other people.

This is certainly what I feel happened in my case. It wasn't supposed to be a kick in the teeth. Rather it was a way of my establishing that I could let go of other people's opinions, as long as I had acted with integrity.

Like most challenges in life, the silver lining is often the important factor.

With Reiki helping us to maintain high levels of self-awareness, we don't need big dramas to be played out in order for us to review who and what we are. We can monitor our reactions and what lessons life is teaching us at every opportunity. Accordingly we often benefit from studying even relatively minor events from several angles. Hence, when I did this, I could sense the opportunity I was being given by The Universe.

Knowing I had a history of self-doubt, there was a realisation that inner growth would be asking me to accept my true worth. Here was an invitation to respond in a different way to how I would have done in the past. From this perspective, these scenarios seemed much more about asking *"Can I approve of myself when others seemingly do not?"*

It was therefore fortunate for my ego (and a very helpful way of bringing this particular message home to me), that I had another of her previous clients come to my clinic. The gentleman concerned continued to come for an appointment every two weeks, for about two years, until his retirement. He commented on how he felt *"we were different, but equally lovely."*

So there we go. You can't be all things to all people. That isn't just Reiki, that's life.

The interesting thing is the order in which the above events happened. The first instance of my inheriting the other therapist's client was the man who thought we were both good Practitioners in our own right, and it happened very soon after I replaced her.

Life Lesson One – It felt like I was being told *"you deserve to be here. You are different but of equal value."*

The woman who gave me the impression that I wasn't giving her sufficient psychic insight, was the second instance, and was more than six months into my term there.

Life Lesson Two – *"Do **you** believe you have value, even when you are different to others?"*

The woman who felt almost nothing, came about six months after that.

Life Lesson Three –*"Do you **really** believe it, to the extent that you can withstand some negative feedback?"*

When she explained she hadn't felt much, at the end of the treatment, she did tell me she was incredibly stressed. She wondered if she hadn't felt much because it was so difficult to relax, having shared some extremely intimate information for the very first time. *"Maybe,"* she said, she was *"unable to relax in the same way as usual?"*

And I thought *"Yes, that could be it, or it could just be that your energy works loads better with someone else"*. I thought it, *and **I felt it**,* and it didn't matter or concern me. Breakthrough moment!

Finally, I wasn't knocking myself down based purely on one person's experience. In times past I could have had twenty clients singing my praises and one not, and guess who I would have focused my attention on?

You know how when we are feeling vulnerable we have one of two responses, by which I mean fight or flight? Well traditionally in such circumstances I would have been ordering my Nike's but with no time to pick them up as I ran away in whatever footwear I currently found myself in. Even should that be the most uncompromising of slingbacks. My feelings used to revolve around the wish to run and hide when under pressure.

Here I was now though, under the intense pressure of being less than expected or hoped for, and yet somehow being okay with that, ignoring my regular impulses and standing in my own power.

Goodness, I'll give myself full marks on the maturity scale for that one.

"How's your self-esteem Sarah?"

"Well coming along nicely, thank you."

(I'd almost finished this book and I've had to come back and add in this paragraph because amazingly the life lesson three client has just contacted me to make another appointment – years after our first. I could have so easily been clinging on to feelings of inadequacy for that entire time, over my perception of her experience. I guess I have just received **Life Lesson Four**.)

Never be put off by someone failing to experience Reiki as you would ideally wish for them to do so; how they feel about Reiki is their business, not yours.

As I've already said, I always look for honesty in my relationship with my clients, and sense that they would be more likely to share their *true* experience if they know there is no right or wrong answer, just their answer. It gives the freedom to a client to explain the wide spectrum of sensations possible during a treatment, from '*nothing*' to '*oh wow*'. This gives them permission to let go of trying meet any perceived expectations.

We just have to accept that sometimes a client's response is not going to be what we hope for. And there may be a range of reasons why you may not get the feedback you would desire...

With Reiki we are going beyond the logical and the conscious mind, and that may be such a big shift for the recipient that they don't feel comfortable talking about their experience. Then again, for whatever reason, some people just don't like to express what's happening for them and in not doing so, give a false impression that that relates to very little. Or they may feel awkward saying it felt as if a pair of hands were working on their feet and ankles whilst we were laying our hands on their shoulders.

The client may not notice changes in their mood or body until long after they have left your company. So if a client looks blankly at you and states they didn't really feel anything, don't be deflated and accept it as failure. Rather allow yourself an open verdict. I've seen such people return, because the positive effects took a while to reveal themselves. It can take several weeks for the energy change to be fully processed and integrated.

As mentioned earlier, we have to accept that on occasions there will never be any *conscious* acknowledgement that the Reiki helped in any way. Humans are complicated and our experiences are working on many different levels. We cannot always be privy to these.

❧ Unfortunately we also have to accept that we just might not be the best fit as a Reiki Practitioner for that individual. Remember that can be the case whilst running any business in life. You can be an excellent hairdresser for instance, but not everyone will come to you for their haircut. You will attract the right customers for you. If a person chooses to go to the salon on the corner rather than yours, it doesn't reflect on your ability to style hair or to please a customer. Allow Reiki clients to have that same flexibility of choice. Matching a person to the right therapist means it won't always be you. (It's an energy thing!)

❧ It may be that you were perhaps a little off balance on that day. No one can be at their best all of the time.

❧ It could be a case of the client's expectations being so overly high that in feeling little, they register it as zero.

❧ It may be that the client is blocking themselves from receiving. I once gave a treatment to a fellow Practitioner and very surprisingly I could feel almost no energy emitting through my hands during the treatment. It was puzzling and most unexpected. Then she kindly told me, about half way through the session that she felt she was blocking the energy and she would try to change this – successfully it seemed as the Reiki then began to feel very strong. Her own Reiki journey will have helped her to notice what was (not) happening, whereas someone new to the process would neither be able to provide that feedback, or know how to change things.

We've spoken already about how people who are stressed or anxious often need to put themselves in control of situations in order to negate those feelings as much as possible. This makes them very analytical in nature; they are in their heads a great deal of the time because it is here that their means of control originates. Those who seek to retain control will typically be more comfortable with an act of giving rather than receiving, and so it may take more than one treatment for them to feel able to let go sufficiently to breakaway from this long entrenched pattern.

Rather than the releasing of physical symptoms, the energy may be helping an individual to handle them differently (better), by taking the client out of a 'victim' state. The condition will remain, but they will be able to handle and cope with it much more successfully. This is unlikely to be instantly recognised.

❀ In a similar vein, whilst a physical condition may continue and medication always be required, treatments may ease or eradicate the side-effects of that medication, bringing relief but not in the way that might have initially been sought.

❀ Finally, Reiki just may not be the right thing for someone full stop.

I'm sure the most helpful attitude to have is a curiosity and interest regarding how a client will respond. This will then mean we're open to whatever is meant to happen for their highest good. Such an outlook can be particularly beneficial where an individual is forming a less obvious relationship with Reiki, such as when it comes into their life temporarily as a beautiful stepping stone, because what they actually need is something else…

One client, let's call her Karen, came for a short series of treatments. She had been diagnosed by her Consultant with a large uterine fibroid which had led him to believe that the best course of action she could take was to have a hysterectomy.

Karen was petrified about surgery. Indeed any hospital procedure terrified her. (I'm right behind you there Karen. Behind you by about another ten meters, hiding behind the pot plant.)

Karen had a series of three treatments with me. As they progressed, it was as if she were becoming more accustomed to do what she actually needed to do to make herself well, which appeared to be, having the operation.

In our first consultation together, she had given me a long list of therapies that hadn't worked for her. I hadn't particularly taken much notice of this until the third session when it suddenly took on more meaning. At this point we were able to conclude that she really had much more trust and faith in orthodox medicine than in any complementary therapy. However, her deep-seated fears had been making her avoid the orthodox path.

It seemed that the Reiki, rather than healing her directly, had taken more of an indirect approach, by bringing her increasing comfort and confidence about the idea of surgery. It appeared likely that this more traditional form of healing was the way in which she would allow herself to regain her health, it being in greater alignment with her beliefs.

You see, here was Reiki giving her what *she needed*. Could she heal in any other way? Of course we can't know. Being open-minded needs you to be open-minded *in all directions*. That can mean accepting a traditional answer, and not feeling you are being open-minded only when you accept a less well-trodden path.

Another client came to me because his partner had felt he would benefit in the ways she was finding that she was. At the end of a couple of treatments I sensed that he really would be best seeking counselling. It was one of those Soul connection nudges, because I didn't receive a particular signal that this would be the case. This was just one of those times (another 'wow' moment), when you say something that you didn't know you were going to, when it doesn't really feel as if it is coming directly from you, and yet once said, you know its value is pure gold.

I spontaneously suggested that he see a counsellor, which my logical mind may well have had a few reservations about voicing. (This type of recommendation could be misconstrued – *"what are you telling me, I need THERAPY?"*). His relief was palpable. He told me that he had long been thinking that this was what he really needed to do.

I was therefore effectively giving him *permission* to go and do what his inner wisdom had been inviting him to do, but that he hadn't felt able to accept.

You may remember a little while back, I mentioned that the inner wisdom we all have *"tends only to whisper, never shout. We have to listen for the quiet voice that speaks from our heart, rather than the loud, shouty one that our head is all too familiar with"*. I believe Reiki connects us more easily to those softly spoken words, but just hearing them is not enough. Can we honour and love ourselves sufficiently to follow them? Sometimes enabling that to happen can be the true art in helping someone to heal.

I know when you are starting out it can more easily feel like a failure to pass a client on to another therapist, so I hope the following analogy will make it easier.

Imagine you are working in a jewellery shop and you love the items you sell. You know that they are all beautifully made, and that they are offered for a fair price. You enjoy it when someone buys from you, because you know that they will love what they have purchased. One day a potential customer comes into the store. They begin to look around, and somehow you can tell that the type of jewellery you offer, will not be what they are looking for. Your items are all in silver, some plain, some with beautiful crystals, but she tells you that she is looking for earrings made of gold. You are never going to be able to satisfy this requirement. This is through no fault of your personality, your shop, or the items that you sell. However in such a situation pleasure can still be found, because you can direct them to a wonderful goldsmith who works around the corner. You see their eyes light up with gratitude that they will likely be able to purchase exactly what they are looking for. You then share that lovely moment when you and they know, that you have understood them, as well as helped them.

If you recommend another therapist with this attitude, you will have a similarly lovely moment to share. Don't talk yourself out of this by telling yourself that Reiki takes the higher ground because it is seemingly more spiritual. I suggest that there is no therapy (and actually no profession) that is without its spirituality.

We benefit when we recognise that one element of being spiritual is in being able to see the beauty in difference, and appreciate the diversity of expression in caring for others.

It is important not to feel that you have all the answers and that anyone who approaches things from another direction is less aware than you. That way, religion and dogma lie, where belief becomes restrictive thinking that *this* is the spiritual way and anything else is either wrong or inferior.

If our Soul's expression is to include becoming a Reiki Practitioner, where would we be without those in the construction industry, or farming? We have not chosen a higher or better path. We have simply chosen that which makes our heart sing. We can take joy from that fact, whilst others can do the same, wherever that may take them. Part of our ability to let go is giving others the freedom to be and do what is right for them.

Doing what is right for them will thankfully be a natural consequence when you just let the Reiki flow, relying on its innate intelligence to free you from any decisions about what you think might be needed, by providing what is actually required. Phew, that's a relief!

There's no requirement to establish which issue to work on first, as neither you nor your clients have to dissect or judge, just allow. Not only does this relieve any stress on your part, it is also a bonus in that you can with integrity claim that the client *heals* themselves. You are not their healer. You are a facilitator of their ability to heal themselves. As such you empower everyone who comes to you.

Hence there are likely to be many times when you can bask in the wonderfulness of hearing how someone's body is healing, in a place you didn't even know was out of balance. Maybe they have come to you because they have been feeling stressed at work, and yet they walk out not only calmer, but on a stronger left knee.

The other day a client came to me, whose emotions were being tested by a challenging life situation. This would have been my focus for healing, if I had tried to be in control of the process. Afterwards, however, she told me how she'd felt the most amazing changes taking place down the right side of her body, where so many of her health issues were! During the Reiki she had felt great changes in her sinus, head, all down her neck – *"oh, didn't I mention that I have compression in my neck?"* – and into her right arm. She felt the changes. Pressure points were being pressed, she heard clicks and movements as the re-balancing took place. She felt tingling all down her arm right to the fingertips...I could go on. As she explained, she was able to confirm that she knew that *she was healing herself*. Surely there can be no better understanding than a client feeling their own power?

Letting go of a preferred outcome also forces you to let go of any responsibility for the degree to which someone heals. Isn't that so spiritual in itself? Reiki says *"here is help, support, assistance and love"* but not at the expense of your own sovereignty.

This is not, by the way, to under-estimate how much you are actively a part of the process. You are instrumental and yet this is a work of collaboration, which takes nothing away from either party. Rather, it understands that we are in essence all one, acting both individually and collectively at the same time.

You are supplying an enhanced sensitivity to a beautiful pure form of energy that they can use to heal themselves whilst increasing their awareness of their Soul-self/spiritual essence.

I suppose it's a little like if you were treating someone who had just cut themselves. You are the one who cleans a wound, puts on the anti-septic and then a plaster to keep it clean, but it's the other person that is actually healing their skin. Without the measures you have taken, the cut may have healed itself, or it may have become infected and worsened. Either way you have certainly provided more of an opportunity for the former to take place.

Wonderful you.

What's There To Fear?

Isn't it wonderful how acts based on love always allow for everyone to benefit? Any act of kindness to another can never require complete self-sacrifice, since, at the very least, it enables the giver to feel good about themselves, and benefit from a healthy dose of self-love.

The loving energy that we know as Reiki definitely follows the understanding that love never divides, it always multiplies. It is a happy circumstance of our work therefore, that we can confirm to those clients concerned we are depleting our energy whilst treating them, that this is absolutely not the case. The energy flows to and for the Practitioner, as well as for its primary recipient.

'Life-force energy' implies that it isn't switched on and off, except at the very start and end of our lives. It is always with us. Therefore Reiki is an act of focusing our awareness on its existence. This makes it all the more extraordinary to me that some people experience fears around its application. I'm forced to ask myself why?

I believe that there are two main reasons. The first relates to the fact that Reiki is, by its nature, a way of opening up an individual to some less-physical realms, together with some less logical aspects of ourselves. There can be implications to this. Secondly, that where we believe in any negativity around Reiki, it is saying far more about ourselves and our relationship to life, than anything else. Our fears are really only about us, and not about Reiki at all. So let's look at each of these in turn.

The metaphysical and intuitive parts of our being, that may have been dormant since birth, can awaken with the touch of Reiki, for example when we feel unexpected sensations or see images during a treatment. It's as though we are being offered a new language of life. So if Reiki were a book, this language, which some people might term as 'psychic' ability, helps us to read the 'book' of Reiki – to experience more of its delights. If we then use that language, (level of consciousness, or psychic capability) in other ways – to read other 'books' (have other psychic life experiences) – the temptation is to merge our understanding of Reiki with the other 'reading' experiences we have, then to claim it is all Reiki, when really it is part of a library that's at our disposal.

For instance, Reiki doesn't ask you to connect with non-physical entities in any way, as part of the process. That said, some people may sense they are doing so. Some teachers may even direct or encourage individuals to connect with what they might term 'guides', 'Ascended Masters' or similar.

Now whether this means truly connecting with that guide or Master, or whether it is with the energy best represented by the qualities attributed to them, is neither my concern nor issue. The point I would like to make is that such a scenario has already brought the person involved out of the central aspect of Reiki. They are already in different territory – reading another 'book' of life. To my mind this is how fears can be introduced to what is designed only to be a completely loving act.

If concerns are raised about who or what other energies could become involved in the process, then it's understandable that this can create a feeling that one needs to protect oneself.

However if we are acknowledging Reiki as our life-force energy, then it isn't anything outside of us; it is our constant companion. As such it is incompatible with concerns regarding its safety. Any instances where we question this will be through issues that we, or our teachers, are bringing to the experience. I feel this should be acknowledged because it is imperative that we don't transfer any thoughts, however minor, of connecting to darker aspects of energy, when working with others.

The act of Reiki is more a turning of our focus towards an ever-present loving energy – opening our awareness to it. When we tell ourselves that we are connecting to it, channelling it and harnessing it for positive purpose (healing), it is effectively focusing our intention to both sense and use it for the highest good, not creating the structure by which it is formed. (Hence my fellow pupil who did Pilates being able to come across it before completing her training.)

The second reason I believe some people experience fears around Reiki, involves the fact that certain aspects of our personalities are fear driven. These traits tend to be represented in every area of our lives. However, we can erroneously associate a new experience with the onset of that fear, rather than as further opportunity to witness it. Accordingly we often fail to see that rather than its being a part of the new environment in which we find ourselves, we've actually brought it with us.

If you have fears around the use of Reiki, ask yourself whether it is stemming from a general lack of security – a feeling that could have been generated through circumstances created in a completely different area of your life. Have you therefore unwittingly brought it with you into this new arena? If so, you could be allowing that lack of security to reveal itself to you *within* the Reiki environment, where 'doing Reiki' has simply given you another dimension in which to play out your life dramas. Reiki can be as much a blank sheet coloured by our thoughts and beliefs, as life is in general.

What do I mean by that? Well, imagine you have a self-esteem issue. There is the opportunity for this vulnerability to be played out just in one, but more likely, in most areas of your life – from work, to family, finances to friendships. In each instance you may be aware of it to either a greater or lesser degree.

When you begin another activity, it could be 'golf', 'charity work', or any other new pursuit, you have effectively created another dramatic stage on which the issue can manifest. It wouldn't be that golf or charity work causes the issue; they simply offer an additional platform from which you can notice it.

Imagine now if you are turning up at the golf club for the first time. You see all the shiny new BMWs and Mercedes lined up in the carpark, and immediately feel inferior in your 10 year old Vauxhall. Someone who is placing their golf clubs in the back of their car, fails to smile or acknowledge you. In your head you've told yourself you're unwanted and won't fit in. You're completely unaware that the person concerned had just received a phone call from his wife. His father has been rushed to hospital – he hasn't even noticed you, let alone ignored you. Your demeanour however, has now changed.

As you enter Reception, noticing you aren't giving off friendly vibes, the Receptionist is terser than usual, perhaps thinking you've probably just arrived in your brand new Porsche, and feel you're above them. You on the other hand believe the exact opposite, feeling as if you've probably have a sign written on your forehead which reads *"second-hand car owner, shouldn't really be here"*. And so it goes on.

The problem lies in seeing this as the Golf Club's fault, when truly it was *your response* to it.

Accordingly when you are overly fearful this can reveal itself *within* the Reiki environment, but it isn't generated by it. The experiences you have as a consequence of doing Reiki will simply be reflecting who you are, back to yourself.

It is therefore paramount to look at the person and not look to blame the energy. That would be like blaming a room for being the wrong colour, when it was you that painted on the emulsion.

Another possible aspect of fear encountered as a Practitioner is that a symptom arises during a course of treatments, and a client wonders if it could have appeared because of the Reiki, or you wonder if you should have done more to have prevented it from appearing in the first place.

In your early days as a therapist, there can be a tendency to feel overly responsible for everything that happens in a client's life once they have walked through your door. Unfortunately you cannot provide 100% protection from all of life's challenges as part of your remit as their Practitioner. A new health condition can arise, even as treatments are on-going. After all, you will be giving yourself Reiki most days, and would not expect to live a life free from any health challenges.

One way which helped me to settle with this situation was to think how a person might see a doctor initially about a peptic ulcer. They wouldn't see any dereliction of care, when the very next week they had to go and see them over an issue with high blood pressure.

It is important to remember that Reiki is actually a system for bringing spiritual self-awareness and a level of holistic balance – mind, emotion and spirit, as well as body. It is not centred on releasing physical health conditions, it's just that this is often a wonderful bi-product.

It's worth taking that into account too, when you are writing any marketing material for your business. No therapy is ever going to be a panacea for life.

That said, Reiki can be a very powerful way of helping someone to heal themselves, to whatever degree that is possible. The very fact that it is the energy helping your client to make the changes, with no massage, manipulation or invasive techniques being used on your part, also ensures it is entirely safe. Even orthodox medicine is increasingly acknowledging its benefits. Our therapy is now readily available on the British National Health Service. It is being used more and more by, and on behalf of, medical staff, from doctors through to midwives.

In fact let me share a lovely endorsement from a Consultant Paediatrician, based at The Royal Alexandra Children's Hospital in Brighton. *"The Reiki treatment has improved sleep, [lessened] fear, anxiety, distress and pain for children on our paediatric critical unit over and above what we can achieve through modern medicine. To have such a fantastic team of people offering Reiki really helps our patients get better quicker."*

When I did some volunteering work at a local hospital, I was informed by the organiser that she routinely receives requests directly from the doctors there. These include asking her to provide Reiki during medical procedures; they recognise that not only does it calm the patient, it also improves their recovery time.

And it's becoming much more common for my clients to tell me that they have come for a session on the suggestion of their doctor. One example of this was a Consultant who suggested it to help his patient (let's refer to him as Mike), suffering with Trigeminal Neuralgia – and suffering is exactly the word to use. Because the condition also goes by the name of *"the suicide disease"*, as very sadly significant numbers of people would rather take their life than live with its excruciating pain.

The trigeminal nerve is primarily responsible for transmitting sensations from the face to the brain. Consequently Mike was finding it difficult to talk and even to eat. The medication he was being given was unable to alleviate his symptoms and his Consultant told him that he had reached the point of requiring surgery as a last resort option.

Then he happened to ask if Mike had ever considered having Reiki, because his wife was a Reiki Master and he felt it might be able to help. This is how Mike came to attend my clinic.

Mike came for an extended series of treatments and it wasn't a situation of constant improvement. Sometimes there would be a relapse and progress would then seem slow, but largely things went in the right direction. I bet you can imagine the total elation we both felt though when all those months later he was telling me that he had become *"pain free"*. There's hardly a better feeling in this world. Fantastic.

As well as being the reason for people seeking out treatments, medical professionals can also be the ones to validate them. For example when a client who had received a series of sessions from me found she was experiencing a further instance of Exploding Head Syndrome. (And yes, I promise you that really is the medical term for a specific condition. Google it.)

Her previous introduction to this syndrome had not been discussed at our initial consultation, mostly because, at that point, she hadn't ever known she'd had it. The reason she told me about it when she did (at the time of her fifth appointment), was because she had almost been late for our session together; this was because she'd come straight from her doctor's surgery.

She went on to explain that the previous night she had been drifting off to sleep, and then been terrifyingly brought around, by an enormous bang that had sounded like a gunshot. Wondering whether she had been transported to the OK Corral, or was still in bed in Hertfordshire, she had been brave enough to get up and examine the evidence. Although she half sensed that the explosion had occurred *inside* her head, and not outwardly at all.

There was no further sign of anything untoward. But due to the ferocity of the event, she had continued to contemplate what had happened. Remembering a similar scenario in her past, she had decided she should visit the doctor to ask if there was any possibility that it could have been self-created.

She recounted how she had fortunately been able to make an appointment with her GP that very morning, just a short time before we were due to meet. She went on to tell me that her doctor had confirmed that she had described a case of Exploding Head Syndrome, which occurs either as you are about to fall asleep, or about to wake.

When her doctor made her diagnosis, my client then asked *"could Reiki have **caused** this to happen?"* That was when her GP went on to explain that Exploding Head Syndrome usually occurs in times of exhaustion. And that Reiki, when it begins working, often makes people feel so much better that they begin to over-do things before they should!

Goodness. I love hearing how practitioners of orthodox medicine are embracing our therapy.

At the time though, it was particularly gratifying, because my client's question to her doctor had sparked a fleeting feeling of unrest in me. *"Could Reiki have **caused** this to happen?"* I've felt I've known the answer since I did my training. No. It can't and won't; but when you are faced with a client asking something similar, you can sometimes notice fears that can be hidden deeply within you – fears that you otherwise might not realise you even possessed.

Discerning the slight disquiet raised in me until the comfort of the doctor's response was shared, I knew there was something I needed to address.

When we use our fears as markers (even when they are subtle and could be easily ignored), using them to question our beliefs so that we can move beyond fear and further into trust, they become very valuable. Unwelcome company I'll grant you. But they are the way in which we know we have an issue to resolve within us. They are the very things that make us look into ourselves and determine who and what we *wish* to be or feel, showing us the next step towards becoming so.

The good news was that I was receiving a gentle message highlighting an area of my beliefs that I needed to amend. With Reiki making us more self-aware, we see what we want to change in ourselves without the need for a big drama to bring it to our attention. I needed to increase my level of trust.

Indeed the nature of our work means we can never be in a complete state of knowing. Trust will always have to play its part. Largely I suspect the absolute truths will evade us until we have passed from this world and into the next. The very nature of our profession means we will have to work to some degree in the unknown. Even what we see and what we sense during a treatment might be only *our way* of experiencing the energy as much as what might actually be happening.

We just can't fully know; and as Gerry Spence once said "*I would rather have a mind opened by wonder than one closed by belief*". So I suggest you get happy with the state of not having all the answers. It will come up in many ways.

In fact thinking back to my client experiencing Exploding Head Syndrome, for the vast majority of us one of those ways will be the number of health conditions you come across that you have never heard of, especially as your client base broadens. Please remember you are not supposed to know them. Reiki is not about being a medical expert. In fact, I often feel a form of freedom when a client mentions a condition, and I say I have absolutely no idea what they are referring to. It's as if I can acknowledge that I will be unbound by what is 'known' about it.

By having no expectations, I can expect anything to happen.

So *never* feel awkward about being open with a client that you are unfamiliar with an ailment – they will respect your honesty which is, after all, the very foundation for your relationship with them. In such circumstances, any clarification from your client will provide you with how *they* are experiencing a condition, which is likely to be far more revealing and helpful to the healing process, than knowing what the general symptoms tend to be.

Whether you're unaware of a condition through lack of medical knowledge on your part, or perhaps because it was not even mentioned by your client in the pre-treatment consultation, of course it just doesn't matter. As pointed out earlier, and no doubt you will recall from your training, the energy will go where it is most needed, and you can be in blissful ignorance about the details.

However, when dealing with overly left-brained people (who may find it more difficult to believe that Reiki is working for them), a little more detail can help their mind settle, or catch-up with some of the physical changes that are being made. It seems that often in such circumstances, I will receive a mental image representing how the energy is working.

For instance, where someone might have an imbalance in their ankle, I may receive images of a golden oil spreading through and around the joint. I am then led to share that image as it manifests. Explaining how the oil is easing movement and improving flexibility, much as car oil will for a motor vehicle's engine. The client has then been provided with a set of images that they can use during the treatment, and beyond. The images confirm the energy is making changes, and allows their mind to agree with what their body already knows.

Where a client's mind is having trouble making sense of the health improvements they can feel in their body, because their mind is grappling with such a seemingly illogical act, or where a long-held condition appears to have released its symptoms with incredible speed, I've noticed it can lead some people to over-test their bodies after the treatment. It's as if they can't find the trust in their minds that their body has altered. Watch out for this.

There'll be times when you have just spent the best part of an hour getting them to relax and allow their body to re-balance itself. They get off the couch telling you *"that feels great, so much better, I can move it much more easily, and almost all the pain has gone"*; but then they go on and on checking that new-found flexibility; whilst they are putting on their shoes, checking, checking; hearing your suggestion for making sure they feel completely alert before they get back in their car, checking, checking; waiting to pay, checking and checking.

You don't want them to be putting back any tension into the muscles when it's only just been released. So if you do find someone who fits this description, notice it on their behalf. They probably won't even realise. Ask them to acknowledge the ease (lovely, that's what you came for), but then retain a level of relaxation that allows their body to continue to heal itself in whatever way it is destined to do.

Client Feedback

Recommendations are a lovely way to generate new clients, but when you are working in such an unusual field as Reiki, they can be a very important way of doing so. They elicit trust in something that might otherwise seem a little on the weird side.

However, there have been far more of my clients letting me know that they have spoken about my skills to their friends and family, than I would have noticed from the numbers of those friends and family walking through my door. This type of healing is patently not for everyone, even when spoken about in glowing terms. In order to make positive feedback work harder for you, I would recommend that you ask for testimonials, so that you can use it for marketing purposes. However, be aware being a member of some professional organisations would prevent you from doing this.

If you specialise in Reiki for those with issues of stress and anxiety then requesting a testimonial can be obstacle. The last thing you want to do is add further pressure to an individual who is already feeling overwhelmed. Accordingly, when I ask, it is only once. And then it must be their choice how to respond, which must include an unpressured opportunity not to.

I've found it feels easier (and it's actually more accurate), to ask for reviews on behalf of other people who may be considering having a treatment, rather than for myself. Suggesting that their review may help someone else to benefit in the ways that they have done feels more comfortable.

I have had clients that have made me feel so sure that they will write one, that I am looking at my phone the next day with the main focus of reading what they have to say, only to find it's nothing. This is where it is important to disconnect a lack of action from your self-worth.

Whilst receiving a positive review is a deliriously happy moment, not doing so is nothing more than an absence of feedback. Avoid letting your mind convince you that it could be anything more than life getting in the way. The client gets home and has ten minutes before the children need picking up from school. One needs to go on to swimming practice, the other needs a careful eye to monitor homework completion. The dinner needs to be prepared and cooked, the dog walked. Life. Life is a busy place and what takes a high priority in your mind, may not be doing so in another's for no other reason than a requirement to fulfil a catalogue of more pressing tasks. It is *not* saying you are not good enough to merit praise.

Whilst the seemingly most enthusiastic of clients may never write you one, there's more than a chance that someone who you felt was agreeing to do so only out of politeness, will surprise you with a beautiful review – one that will touch your heart and bring an emotional tear to your eye.

Be patient, too.

There have been times when many months have gone by, and then all of a sudden a testimonial comes my way, from someone I haven't thought about or seen in ages.

Might I suggest that you ask, then simply leave your energy 'open' to receive a review, if it ever happens and whenever that may be? This way you won't start a conversation with yourself, filling your head with negative self-talk, by trying to justify inactivity as representing a lack of ability on your part.

Of course you have to be prepared to hear some responses that are going to throw you off balance a little. A lovely woman who came for a taster appointment, made all the right noises as she was leaving. Saying how well she felt afterwards, and how she would be back for a full session in the near future.

Personally I don't ask for testimonials until someone has received at least two sessions of Reiki from me. I sense that this timescale will provide both a truer response and fuller feedback. The only reason I received feedback on this occasion was therefore because of the follow-up text message I sent her the next day. Her subsequent reply included the comment that she had found the Reiki "*disconcerting*".

Reiki isn't to everyone's taste, but then I don't like celery – have I mentioned that before?

The sensations in my body which make me go "*wow*" with an almost unrivalled excitement and pleasure can be off-putting or scary if viewed differently. Which brings to mind a regular client of mine who comes for a treatment approximately every eight weeks or so. On her tenth appointment, she told me afterwards how she had been unsettled by the feeling of pressure, (one of *my* wow sensations), which she had felt on her chest, whilst I was over her ankles. To calm her nerves, she had to tell herself she had a cat sitting on her, and then imagined pushing it off, so that it went away.

Now my pre-treatment consultation would usually include the possibility that pressure might be felt, even where my hands were not resting on their body. This, coupled with my enthusiasm for the experience, might well have allayed her concerns, but it was probably such a long time since that introductory conversation, that she would not have been prepared for the event, and remembered no reference to such a likelihood. My *"wow"* was her *"what on earth is that?"*

It seemed that my taster client, whom I might have expected would be very positive *because* she had such physical responses, was actually put off by them. The time restrictions surrounding these type of sessions meant a reduced treatment introduction. This was exacerbated by her need to leave without the usual post-Reiki de-brief, because she was rushing to pick up her children from school. It meant no opportunity to give a better context for her experiences.

All this goes to show that you have to believe in yourself. Testimonials and positive feedback are an added bonus. We have to be confident in our own skills and the effectiveness of the energy, without insisting on validation from others.

This approach is very liberating, especially when working with sceptics which is something that the rebellious part of my nature loves to do.

Hopefully your teacher has confirmed that there is no need for the recipient to believe in Reiki in order for it to work. Primarily it does so because it *is*. It isn't something that has been created in our minds. It doesn't therefore require both parties to agree to believe in its existence. I take you back to my Reiki Level One, and the woman who delivered Reiki energy to her Pilates' students, without any prior knowledge of it. Reiki, or at least what we are commonly labelling it, is a reality, not a figment of a new-age mind.

People have often said to me *"Oh, you have to believe in it for it to work don't you?"* No. That really isn't the case. If someone comes to you and they are open-minded, that is enough. I have had friends who have been really doubtful that Reiki can help them in anyway. They feel as if they are indulging me by accepting my offer to see if it can help them. Then they tell me the next day how their back feels better than they would ever have thought possible and consequently they have had to completely review their stance on what I do for a living. (It's worth remembering too, that if Reiki only worked through some kind of mutual agreement in its existence, then it would fail to explain how it works so beautifully with animals.)

I do however also believe that we each have full sovereignty over our own minds and our bodies. If a person is adamant that Reiki is clap-trap, then I sense that they would be able to block it and *prove to themselves* that it isn't real. That is the prerogative of anyone. An individual is always autonomous, which is as it should be.

Thus the specific energy of the recipient is naturally going to be instrumental in a session's outcome. It's never just down to you and your Reiki skills. Remember this when progress doesn't appear forthcoming, even in the midst of client positivity. I've noticed if a client holds an unrealistically high expectation of what Reiki might do for them (particularly if they are unwilling to put any effort into changing themselves – their behaviour or emotions –

in anyway), advancements may not be forthcoming. Some people want Reiki to be like waving a magic wand. Although it can sometimes appear to be almost as enchanted as that, the attitude and actions of the person concerned will play an important factor in what occurs.

A client's energy can have other implications. I know it is just a fact of life that sometimes we feel "in the flow" and at the top of our game whilst at others, the exact opposite. There will be instances when you raise the bar in your pre-treatment consultation; you would wish a passing video camera was filming the event to be replayed as a shining example of how best to handle every aspect, from rapport building, to treatment explanation, to client empowerment. Other times... not. It can be interesting to observe how these extremes can simply be revealing good or less good days for your performance, but may also be down to your client's energy influencing the situation. I can have been on a trajectory of magnificence (well, making a good job of things anyway) with one client, only to suddenly be feeling unworthy, inconsequential, flat, you name it, a whole gamut of deflationary emotions, just as my next client is approaching. Knowing that I won't have changed my feelings so quickly for no good reason, I've realised that I'm tapping into my next *client's* energy – feeling *their* feelings.

Please note this is *not* about us taking on any of their energy. Nor is it about them overcoming ours in anyway. It's simply the case that as we become more proficient at sensing energy, we often find that we can 'read' someone's emotions more easily. With these senses heightened as we do our work, we need to understand how they can then unexpectedly affect us.

It's not that unusual a skill; most people can tell when a friend is feeling cross or unhappy, well before they have said anything. This ability is simply honed in our job, to the point where sometimes we can do it before we've even met the other person involved.

So be aware, as an energy worker, there can be ways in which you are affected by your clients, which perhaps you hadn't considered. It can be a fascinating part of working in this field.

Working With Young People

Now I said I would include some information on working with young people. It's worth starting by highlighting some of the advantages of our therapy, that you could focus on when discussing with any interested parents:

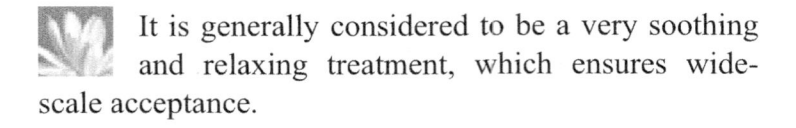

- It is generally considered to be a very soothing and relaxing treatment, which ensures wide-scale acceptance.

- Treatments can take place in the company of the parent, without compromising the benefits.

- Reiki requires no discussion. If a young person finds it difficult or impossible to express their feelings, this offers no barrier to the efficacy of the treatment.

- There is no age restriction and is therefore appropriate for babies upwards.

- It is entirely natural – no drugs or invasive techniques are involved. It is therefore completely safe.

- Reiki works in harmony with other therapies.

- Thoughts of 'therapy' can be replaced with 'relaxation technique'.

I've already mentioned some additional considerations and guidelines to follow in the section covering working with clients that require supervision. But in case you are reading this in isolation, here's a repeat of the points covered.

- There are legal guidelines effecting the treatments of those deemed to be children (under sixteen years of age) in the eyes of the law in the UK. There are likely to be comparable requirements in whichever country you operate. Accordingly I ask the parent or guardian to sign and date a typed document which specifies the following:

> *"A parent or guardian who wilfully fails to provide adequate medical aid for a child under the age of sixteen, may be committing a criminal offence. Reiki is not defined as a medical aid by law, so anyone who treats a child whose parents refuse medical aid, could be seen to be aiding and abetting that offence.*
>
> *I have been warned by Sarah Cooper that, according to law, I must consult a doctor concerning the health of my child."*

This is to cover any situations where medical intervention is the appropriate course of action and a complementary therapy should be just that – complementary to orthodox medicine.

When working with younger children I believe it is necessary for the parent or guardian to accompany the child during all treatments. With teenagers I am happy for a second appointment to run without chaperoning, if this is sought by both parties. This is usually the case once they know what to expect. It can be helpful in enabling the young person concerned to open up about some of the reasons behind their stress or worries.

In the case of young children I suggest to the parent that they bring a toy, particularly a soft toy that can be cuddled during the treatment. It can also be a great access point to receiving the child's feedback on how the session went – much less threatening to ask how the teddy bear felt!

I ensure it's understood that it's likely the Reiki will likely affect *all* those in the room, and not just the main recipient.

A treatment is likely to run for less than the standard hour. Usually a child's body language will tell you that they've had enough as they go from being relaxed to restless, often after about forty minutes and it may be as little as twenty five. I adapt (reduce) my fee, relative to the time involved in each instance.

I hope the following short case studies will provide a few examples of how Reiki may help younger people:

Child A – seven years old.

When Child A's mother contacted me to make an appointment, I suggested that he bring a favourite soft toy or similar to hold during the treatment.

On meeting the child I ensured that I was introduced to the toy and that I knew its name.

We spoke a little about things he likes doing (colouring and football) to build rapport.

When explaining what was about to happen, I spoke about changing "unhappy feelings into happier feelings" rather than talking about energy changes.

During the treatment I asked Child A several times if he were comfortable and happy to continue.

The treatment lasted just under forty five minutes. Afterwards I asked what both Child A and the child's toy felt about the session. Child A confirmed that they had both "liked it". Child A looked noticeably more relaxed at the time of leaving.

Child B – twelve years old.

Child B first came for a Reiki treatment when she was twelve years old.

She was brought to the appointment by her mother, who explained that she was looking for her daughter to feel more calm and relaxed, and to be happier in herself.

Child B did not speak until after the treatment when she said that she had been able to become *"very relaxed"*.

Child B returned for a treatment two weeks later. She was confident enough to come to the treatment room on her own. She felt sufficiently comfortable to tell me that:

- She felt *"nice"* from the last treatment.
- Calmer.
- She gave me an example of her behaviour from the previous week. When she had asked to play with a friend and her mother had said no, Child B had just said *'okay'* and accepted her mother's decision. In the past whenever her mother said *'no'* to her, she told me she would get cross, angry and argue about it.

Approximately one year later I received a phone call from Child B's mother who said that her daughter had requested a Reiki treatment with me because *"It really worked last time."*

Child B returned for two further treatments and said that since the first session she:

- ❖ Felt Calmer.
- ❖ Was sleeping better at night.

Child C – fifteen years old.

Child C attended with her mother.

At the start of the first session her mother explained in Child C's presence, that Child C was neither happy, nor content. *"She smiles a lot but this hides how she is feeling. She is depressed."*

Child C said nothing before the treatment but afterwards remarked on the warmth of the energy during the session.

Child C attended for a second session two weeks later. This time she asked her mother to remain downstairs.

Child C said that she had felt a lot better after the treatment for the next few days, but that this had worn off. I explained how this is normal, and it can take a few treatments for the effects to be longer-term. She said that today wasn't a good day, she was angry, she hadn't done well in her exams and that her cat had died and that *"he was her friend"*.

She said she didn't think she would be able to relax as much as last time. However during the treatment she relaxed sufficiently to fall asleep.

After the treatment she remarked how much tension had left her muscles, especially around her jaw and neck area and she looked much brighter.

Child C attended a third session and told me that the good feelings from the Reiki had lasted longer after second session than the first one. She showed interest in what Reiki is about, and what it feels like to give Reiki. She has begun to show interest in being at school, and her general outlook on life is far more positive.

Reiki has appeared to be a wonderful resource to help young people through difficult times. Whether that is down to family break-ups, exam pressure, or simply the emotional turmoil that most of us have contended with as part of growing up. Providing a young person's connection to Reiki has always felt like the most tremendous privilege.

Some Final Thoughts

And Finally...

For all the attention we have paid to the multi-faceted relationship we will have with our clients, at the end of the day, the one constant in working with Reiki, is going to be ourselves.

A key part of being the best Reiki Practitioner you can be, is going to be based upon how you treat yourself. If your focus is constantly on others then there will be something missing in your business; a fundamental part that should lie at the heart of all you do; that is your health and well-being, your self-care and self-love.

After all, if we want our clients to find these things, we're duty bound to show them the way. We won't be perfect, any more than our clients will be, but if we are seeking for them to love themselves more, we need to be in sync with that message, thus ensuring we are acting with integrity.

We need to show kindness to ourselves, to be a source of encouragement and support, inwardly as well as outwardly. We need to make the relationship we have with that voice inside our heads, everything that we would provide to those that ask for our services.

We need to be a friend to ourselves.

Self-Reiki can help to get you there, but it also takes a commitment to use all that is available for improving our levels of self-love, understanding and forgiveness, mirroring what we intend to provide for our clients.

To this end, Reiki "Shares" with other Practitioners are a great benefit, providing the opportunity for both energy exchange and reciprocal mentoring. Also occasional treatments from therapists of different disciplines can be a wonderful way of investing in self-care. Both offer the added bonus of placing yourself in your client's shoes, and you may gain insights from experiencing how other people work. You may take note of things you wish to replicate in your own business, or maybe things to avoid when seen from the recipient's point of view. It also ensures that you only ever ask your clients to do what you are willing to do yourself.

As we become more used to giving treatments there can be a tendency to consider ourselves as the "giver". Too much of that and we become out of balance. We then lose touch with our ability to fully surrender and let go in the hands of another, weakening our ability to trust.

Let's not forget that Reiki is calling us to address and work through our own issues. Using the skills of others can help us on our way. Attending workshops, courses and retreats, or reading what others have to say, helps us to change our emotional frequency in positive ways. It helps us to grow and meet the challenges in our lives, whilst acting as a blueprint for others to do the same.

Raising our energy vibration can act as a beacon attracting others and encouraging them. Allowing us to radiate a message of hope and love, when others feel lost.

So the final message of this book is to ask you to love yourself.

With love, Sarah x

Thank you so much for reading this book. I hope that you have gained value from doing so, as it would give me great pleasure to think that in some small way I may have helped you on your own Reiki journey.

If you feel able to leave a positive review on Amazon, however short, that would be simply amazing – thank you.

Also, if you can, please recommend this book to fellow Practitioners, or your Reiki students. It's always lovely to share knowledge and support others wherever possible…

Sarah Cooper lives in the county of Hertfordshire in England. She loves the beauty of the natural world, and becomes deliriously happy when looking at rainbows, sunsets, or gazing at stars in the night sky. She is also known for becoming overly excited at the sight of snowflakes.

Printed in Great Britain
by Amazon